COOKING WITH
CHIA

COOKING WITH
CHIA

NICKY ARTHUR

NEW
HOLLAND

To my mum and dad, who showed me how to live a simple life and appreciate organically-grown vegetables.

Also to my daughters Lucia and Millijana, who bring me love and joy every day.

Acknowledgements

The things I value and treasure most in my life, which I call the 'big rocks', are my two daughters. I would like to acknowledge Lucia and my baby Millijana and their father, Jud, because if it wasn't for them I may have never experienced the joy of being a mum, and learning to create healthy meals for the family. Their enthusiasm kept the energy high and the dream alive.

I would like to thank Fiona Schultz and Lliane Clarke at New Holland for believing in me and giving me this opportunity to write *Cooking with Chia*.

Thank you Jacinda, David, Holly and Giles for putting up with my weird and wonderful creations during the month I spent at your home, creating this book.

Thank you to Kapai Puku seeds for supporting me and supplying me with your wonderful seeds. Thank you Graeme and Nina for your support.

Thank you to my friends who have supported me and put up with my excitement of sharing my homemade recipes. To Maggie and Rosie and your big warm loving family of babysitters and being there for us girls.

To my editors Phillipa, Maggie and Audrey for your wonderful styling ideas and Graeme Gillies, who I enjoyed working with the week of the shoot. To all my dream team the week of the photo shoot, Sue, Colleen, Emma, Audrey, Kim, Julyanne, Christina, your time was appreciated and I couldn't have done it without your help. Thank you to my graceful neighbor Vicki for all your crockery and helping out with missing ingredients over the years.

To Linda my agent thank you for your support and believing in me right from the start. I love your energy and wisdom, thank you.

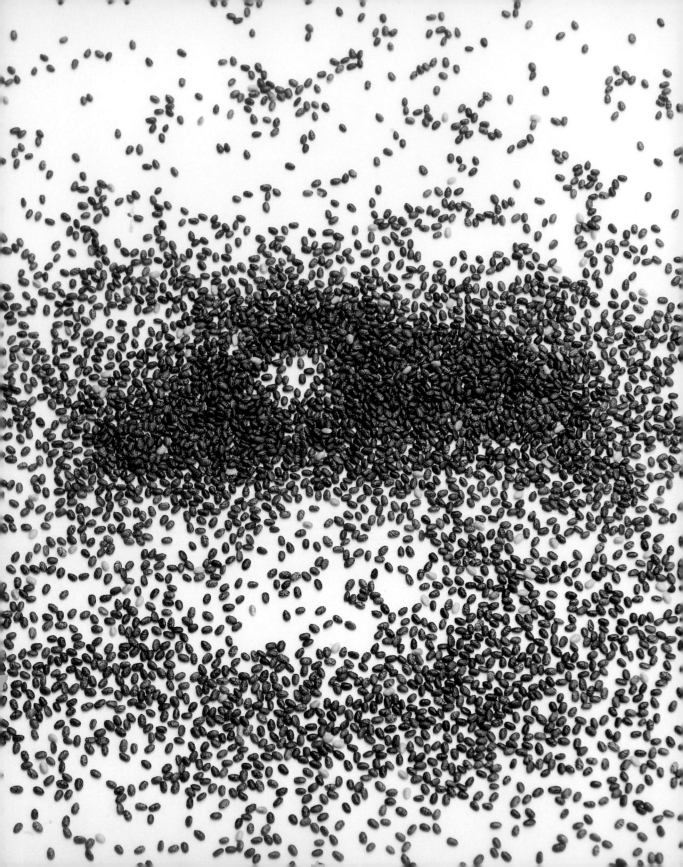

Contents

Introduction

'Let food be thy medicine and medicine be thy food' – Hippocrates

There are things that remain with you from childhood. One of mine is the happy and fun times I had growing up with six amazing aunties. I remember well their baking and our family get-togethers with plenty of food. The other is growing up with organic vegetables from my dad's vegetable garden. I appreciate the simple lifestyle my mum and dad brought me up on, the memories of the apple trees in the backyard and the huge vegetable garden and tomato house. The good old days with my horse in the backyard while dad dug in the garden, listening to his country western music, and mum watering the flowers, are still with me today.

I also grew up close to my Nana Barnes, and most days after school all the family would meet in her tiny warm kitchen and enjoy her scones and biscuits. They were the simple days when no technology distracted us from cooking and playing outside.

I never dreamed I would write a cookbook. However, when one is passionate about what one loves to do, anything is possible. I have spent years trying to create healthier recipes and this opportunity gave me the time to focus solely on creating recipes with the wonder seed, chia.

Becoming a mother and a wife brought a creativity and joy I never realised I had. When I first became a mum my cooking was bland and boring. My husband got used to the same old salad and fish most nights. Every now and then I would get a little creative, but most times I reverted back to what I knew.

I began a raw vegan lifestyle a few years ago. Eating a raw food diet is a complete lifestyle, one that has opened up a whole new world for me in terms of taste, flavour, colour and texture. The super grains and seeds we use in this book will keep your body fuelled, energised and healthy. Most importantly, it's a healing way of life.

Even though I try to eat raw vegan most of the time, I have included some easy-to-prepare cooked dishes and some popular meat dishes for you meat lovers so that you can try the wonder seed that is chia.

To me, simple food equals vibrancy, energy and flavour. It is in our nature to experiment with food, and nature provides for us in abundance, to fuel the body and give us longevity. But too often food is overcooked and processed.

I believe incorporating live seeds like chia and other super grains like quinoa will take you on a path of a more enlightened life. Why? Because you are bringing life back into your body!

I enjoy unlimited creativity when planning and preparing food. And there is significantly less fuss involved – it takes less time and it helps heal and renew the internal body.

Research shows we are in the grip of an epidemic of diet-related illnesses, such as diabetes and cardiovascular disease, which affects up to 65 per cent of the western adult population, not to mention childhood obesity and mental health issues such as depression.

Many people ask if my girls are on a raw food diet. I believe that while they are growing they need variety in their diet, and so I aim for 80 per cent raw food as much as possible. The girls still have the occasional vegetable bake, mashed potato or bolognese. I also get asked how I find time to prepare all this food for my family every day. To be honest, it's less fuss, fewer pots and pans to wash and it takes less time. These days I echo the sentiments of many when I say I'm very busy. I have less time to prepare and cook for my girls than ever before but I still manage to throw a beautiful 'gourmet' raw food recipe together that only takes a few minutes to prepare.

Most of the recipes are dairy and gluten free, while a few use eggs. The milk used in most of the recipes is rice or almond and the gluten-free flours are more nutritious and healthier than conventional flour. You may pay a little more for them, but you will find you only need a small amount. If you have to spend a little more for a healthier choice, consider it an investment in your body. It's worth it.

Why Raw Food?

Living foods provide life-force. By integrating raw living foods into our lives, we can look forward to wellness, greater energy and mental clarity, a positive outlook on life and spiritual awakening.

Living foods are highly rejuvenating. Plant-based foods in their original, un-heated (uncooked) state are raw and alive. These foods include fruits, vegetables, grains, nuts, seeds, seaweed and fresh juices. When prepared, uncooked or in a special dehydrated food dryer at less than 48°C/118°F, they retain the vital life-force nutrients (vitamins, minerals, amino acids, oxygen) and live enzymes required to digest food, repair cellular damage and create billions of healthy new cells every day.

Living foods provide the maximum amount of energy with minimal bodily effort, and research suggests they can help protect against heart disease, diabetes and some cancers. These nutrient-rich foods are also effective in treating allergies, digestive disorders, weak immune systems, high cholesterol, obesity and weight problems, as well as psychological, emotional and skin disorders. Of course I always choose organic produce whenever I can.

The Secrets of 'Unfussy' Cooking

This way of eating satisfies the palate and the best part is that with fewer components and fewer steps, it's less work and is easier to prepare when you're time-poor – simplicity at its best! It's never going to be as easy as opening a can and microwaving something, but it will be better for you.

A commitment to raw food and a healthy eating lifestyle can become habit. It becomes a life all about fruits, vegetables, nuts and seeds. And the seed we focus on in this book is the wonderful chia seed.

This way of cooking is a 'lifestyle' and I promise it will unleash your creativity and energy to create 'gourmet', restaurant-quality flavours.

Although I like to create lots of recipes, I'm aware that food is seasonal. We eat an abundance of what is in season, knowing that there will be something different next season. Nature provides the seasons this way for a reason. Just stop and think for a moment how often you eat the same old thing over and over again. Eat a wide variety of fresh, seasonal produce and you will find that you won't crave. If you do crave, take it as a sign your body is deficient and it may be time to change some habits.

"Society is never more aghast than at a new display of commonsense." George Bernard Shaw

Seasonal produce ensures we are getting a varied diet that is sustainable. You can sustain this way of life because it is rewarding and easy and most of the food is available locally.

This lifestyle has another benefit. You will lose weight and increase your energy and vitality. As I mentioned earlier, most of the food in this book is gluten and dairy free. But it's also sugar and wheat free. Although there are some recipes that you'll need to cook, most of the dishes are prepared without using heat to preserve the nutritional value. Rather than cooking and destroying nutrients we use various cooking techniques, such as blending, processing, freezing and dehydrating. The milk can be made at home from nuts or you can purchase rice and almond milk.

I recycle all my bottles and jars for homemade sauces and chutneys. It is a wonderful feeling to know I can do my bit for the environment. Mindfulness in looking after our planet extends beyond the way we eat and prepare our food.

Ingredients for the Pantry

There are ingredients that form the base of many of the sauces, dips and desserts in this book so it's a good idea to stock up on some of the basics. The basics are fruits, vegetables, nuts, seeds, sprouted grains, oils, spices, and condiments made from natural ingredients. To be more specific:

• Chia seeds: you can order chia seeds in bulk in a 1kg/2lb container, or they can be found at most supermarkets.

• LSA, or almond meal

• Coconut oil

• Agave syrup

• Raw cashew nuts

• Almonds

• Walnuts

• Sweeteners: I use maple syrup and also agave syrup. This is produced from the agave plant from South America. Low glycemic index agave is absorbed slowly into the bloodstream. It's readily available in delicatessens, health food stores and supermarkets.

• Seeds: I also use seed blends which you can buy online. Kapai Puku is one I use often.

• Nutritional yeast: Nutritional yeast is a deactivated yeast, sold in flakes or as powder. It's a Vitamin B boost you can add to soups and breads.

• Flours: I use quinoa flour or make my own oat flour, but blending whole oats.

• Freekeh: this a cereal food made from green wheat that goes through a roasting process in its production. This is a great substitute for pasta.

• Maca powder: Maca is made from a Peruvian root and is a dense super-food that contains high amounts of minerals, vitamins, enzymes and essential amino acids. It is rich in B vitamins and a vegetarian source of B12 and offers amazing energy boost. It helps balance our hormones, which regulate many things including mood growth, sexual development and tissue function and is beneficial for all sorts of hormonal problems including PMS, menopause and hot flushes.

• Add fresh herbs and spices, preferably fresh, to your recipes wherever possible. I have really enjoyed getting to know herbs and spices and using them to add variety and flavour. I have a wide variety on hand and I grow basil, mint, coriander, oregano and rosemary.

Preparing Your Nuts and Seeds

Many of the recipes require you to soak the nuts before blending. This process helps the nuts to break down more easily in the digestive system and will result in a smoother texture. Many recipes will suggest that nuts be soaked for 1–2 hours. However, I have been known to whip up a dish and only soak the nuts for 30 minutes and it has still worked well. The idea is to plan ahead, use this book and decide what you want to make and prepare your nuts and seeds. The beauty of working with chia seeds is that they never need to soak long. When using chia for a gel, a replacement for egg, or as a texture, or to form the gel consistency for drinks or cakes, it only takes a couple of minutes. I also use Kapai Puku seed blends which are available online.

Protein

Often we are programmed to think our only source of protein is from animals. However, the body can get enough protein from a wide and varied diet consisting of nuts, seeds, vegetables, fruits, grains, legumes, and lentils.

All kinds of seeds, including chia, sunflower, pumpkin, sesame and hemp, pine nuts, raw nuts, quinoa, green vegetables, sprouted legumes, tahini, spirulina, sprouted buckwheat, cacao powder, olives and tofu, are excellent sources of protein.

Oils and Cheese

Coconut oil has many health benefits and contains lauric acid, a 'miracle' compound because of its unique health promoting properties. Choose virgin coconut oil and avoid the transfats that can be introduced in the refining process. Goat's cheese contains less lactose than cow's milk. It's lower in calories, easier to digest and is low in sodium.

Tools of the Trade

- High-quality sharp knife
- Fine mesh strainer
- Cutting board
- Measuring cups

Blender or processor

In the past I only used the blender for making protein shakes—in order to get protein from powders. Looking back, I can see how deprived my body was from not including enough wholesome plant-based foods. I love chia as not only do I know I'm getting an abundance of omega-3 but I'm also keeping my joints healthy. I have coped with the smallest processor that worked well, but after trying the efficient blenders and processors available, they really do make it easier. A blender may be used for processing but it is not optimal. A blender is used to emulsify foods. A processor is used to mix ingredients and prepare crusts, flours, pestos, dips or anything that will retain some texture. The base of all my cooking is done with a processor, with a blender for the soups and smoothies.

Dehydrator

I have used an oven, as opposed to a dehydrator, to keep it as simple as possible. Dehydrators are inexpensive though, and are easy to use. You can also use an oven on a lower temperature.

A New Mindset

Creating change in the kitchen and your lifestyle can play games with your mind. In yoga we call this 'the monkey mind'. That is, the mind that flits from thought to thought often telling you 'it's all too hard', 'I don't have any time', 'I can't be bothered', 'I am not creative enough or good enough'. This is what I call a 'negative mindset'. These are self-limiting beliefs and they will stop you from experiencing an amazing and rewarding way of life. I am passionate about teaching healthy living and often it is mindset and a lack of resources that can get in the way.

This book will not only give you some healthy yummy recipes to cook with chia, but also some resources and ideas to help your healthy lifestyle.

Common Measurements

1 teaspoon/tsp = 5g/5ml

1 tablespoon/tbsp = 15g/15ml

30ml = 1fl oz

30g = 1oz

What is Chia?

These days, chia is referred to as a 'superfood', but this tiny seed packed with essential nutrients has its roots in the culture of Mexico and South America, where it has been prized for thousands of years for its health-giving properties.

Chia is a species of flowering plant and part of the mint family. It grows to around a metre high, with purple or white flowers. Chia is grown commercially for its super seed, which is rich in omega-3 fatty acids. By weight chia contains more omega-3 than salmon.

The seeds, which are small in size and coloured brown, grey, black and white, yield 25–30 per cent extractable oil including a-linolenic acid (ALA). The seed is tasteless but adds texture and has the ability to bring flavours out in other foods. Chia may be eaten raw, as in many of the recipes I have created, providing fats and fibre.

Chia can also be soaked in water, after which if becomes gelatinous, making it perfect to use in nutritious and filling drinks. This gel-like consistency makes chia an easy substitute for eggs and butter in puddings, pancakes, breads and cakes.

Chia also contains the essential minerals phosphoros, manganese, calcium, potassium and sodium.

Research shows chia has a range of health benefits which may assist in managing certain conditions, including cardiovascular disease, arthritis, obesity, skin problems and even anti-aging.

Omega 3 is also important for cholesterol and heart health. It's rich in linolenic acid, which has been shown to reduce inflammation. It's also important for brain health and normal growth and development, so great to give the kids.

When you eat a diet high in starchy foods or sweets, blood sugar levels can drop after meals. Do you know that late-afternoon energy slump? Adding chia to your food or drink will turn your body into a powerhouse where a steady flow of energy all day can be sustained, instead of the ups and downs.

Chia also keeps you regular and helps to keep food moving through your digestive system.

One of nature's highest plant-based sources of complete protein, chia helps provide energy, vitamins, minerals and helps balance blood sugar levels, which is especially important if, like me, you don't get protein from animal sources.

Another great advantage of chia is that it allows you to bake with less fat. You can substitute this wonder seed for butter and oil in baking. You will notice I have tried my hardest to cook without dairy and oil in most of these recipes.

Smoothies & Drinks

Add a super-food booster to your smoothies:

Chia seeds – For added omega-3, rich in iron and calcium. To help with joint care and strong heart

Wheat grass – Alkalizing, chlorophyll-rich, detoxifier

Coconut oil – Great fat metaboliser and even increases metabolic rate

Barley grass – Powerful cleanser with minerals

Spirulina powder – Plant-based supplement with protein and amino acids, helps increase energy

Sweet Zucchini Chia Smoothie

Serves 2

2 zucchinis/courgettes
2 apples
1 stalk celery
1 tablespoon fresh ginger
½ lemon
1 scoop spirulina powder
2 tablespoons chia seeds

Juice all ingredients, except chia seeds.

Add chia seeds and spirulina powder and shake or stir well. Add ice as an option. This is best to drink fresh.

Liver Cleanser Smoothie

Serves 1

1 beetroot, peeled
1 stalk celery
2 carrots
2 apples
1 tablespoon ginger, peeled
2 tablespoons chia seeds

Juice all ingredients, except the chia seeds.

Pour into a glass, add chia seeds and stir well.

Mint Chia Smoothie

Serves 1

1 cup rice milk or almond milk

10 fresh mint leaves

1 teaspoon cacao powder

1 teaspoon chia seeds

1 tablespoon agave syrup

1 tablespoon virgin coconut oil

½ vanilla bean

Ice

Blend all ingredients until smooth.

Green Kale Smoothie

Serves 2

2 cups water

1 frozen banana

2 cups fresh spinach, chopped

1 leaf kale

1 tablespoon chia seeds

1 tablespoon spirulina powder

Use a high speed blender. Add water first, then banana, greens and seeds. Blend on high for 60 seconds and add the spirulina. Green smoothies keep really well in the refrigerator for up to 48 hours.

This mint chia is a refreshing and filling snack.

I always have bananas in my freezer ready to go for a green smoothie.
Peel the skin before placing in the freezer. Kale is a superstar when it
comes to carotenoids and flavonids, which are two powerful anti-oxidants.
Like chia seeds, kale is high in omega-3 and helps with inflammatory-related
problems such as arthritis, autoimmune diseases and asthma. Kale is also rich
in vitamin K, Vitamin A for healthy bones and teeth, detoxification and
vitamin C. Add a dose of kale to your smoothies to improve your immune
system and overall health.

Berry Bang

Serves 1

1 cup frozen mixed berries
1 frozen banana
1 cup almond milk
1 tablespoon chia seeds

Blend all ingredients until smooth.

Chia Café Latte

1 cup black coffee

1 vanilla bean

1 tablespoon raw organic cacao powder

1 tablespoon chia seeds

1 frozen banana

1 teaspoon maca powder (optional)

1 teaspoon agave syrup

1 cup almond milk

Blend all ingredients well.

Maca is made from a Peruvian root and is a dense super-food that contains high amounts of minerals, vitamins, enzymes and essential amino acids. It is rich in B vitamins and a vegetarian source of B12 and offers amazing energy boost. It helps balance our hormones, which regulate many things including mood growth, sexual development and tissue function and is beneficial for all sorts of hormonal problems including PMS, menopause and hot flushes.

Mango Magic

Serves 1

1 cup almond milk
1 mango, peeled and sliced
1 tablespoon chia seeds
juice of ½ lemon
1 vanilla bean
½ cup ice

Blend ingredients into a smoothie.

Mango Slushie

Serves 2

2 frozen mangoes, peeled and chopped
1 tablespoon chia seeds
¼ cup water
½ cup ice

Blend all ingredients until smooth.

This one is my daughters' favourite drinks after a hot day. You need a little water to help it blend well.

Energy Booster

Serves 2

1 apple
1 stalk celery
1 leaf kale
1 cup spinach
juice of ½ lemon
juice of 1 orange
1 tablespoon chia seeds
1 frozen banana
2 cups water
1 tablespoon spirulina powder

Blend all ingredients well. Add ice and serve.

Barley grass, wheat grass and spirulina are alkalising, which reduces inflammation and helps prevents cancer, arthritis, diabetes and cardiovascular disease. Chia seeds also help reduce inflammation.

Maca Lucia

Serves 2

2 kale leaves
2 stalks celery
1 tablespoon chia seeds
1 pear
1 teaspoon maca powder
2 cups water

Blend all ingredients well. Serve with ice.

Maca is made from a Peruvian root and is a dense super-food that contains high amounts of minerals, vitamins, enzymes and essential amino acids. It is rich in B vitamins and a vegetarian source of B12 and offers amazing energy boost. It helps balance our hormones, which regulate many things including mood growth, sexual development and tissue function and is beneficial for all sorts of hormonal problems including PMS, menopause and hot flushes.

Breakfast

Citrus Chia Granola

Serves 4–6

1 apple, peeled, cored and chopped
½ cup maple syrup
2 teaspoons vanilla extract
2 tablepoons chia seeds
2 teaspoons ground cinnamon
½ teaspoon sea salt
juice of 2 mandarins (or orange)
1 tablespoon mandarin zest
1 tablespoon lemon zest
1 cup almonds, soaked 3–8 hours
1 cup walnuts soaked for 3–8 hours and
   drained
½ cup pumpkin seeds
½ cup sunflower seeds
1 cup raisins
1 cup cranberries
Honey Lucia (see Breakfast)

Add apple, maple syrup, vanilla, half the chia seeds, cinnamon, sea salt, mandarin juice and zests to the food processor, blend until chunky. Be careful not to over-blend the mixture. It should be in very fine pieces but not pureed. Add to a large bowl. Process nuts until chunky, add to the bowl with the chia mixture.

Add seeds, raisins, cranberries and remaining chia seeds; mix all ingredients until well combined. Store in refrigerator to allow the flavours to blend overnight. Serve with sliced banana and drizzle flaxseed oil or Honey Lucia on top.

This is a recipe for the whole family and will keep well in your refrigerator for 4–5 days. Add a chopped banana or strawberry and sprinkle more chia seeds on top and you have yourself a very nutritious satisfying breakfast or snack.

Honey Lucia

Makes ½ cup

½ cup honey
2 tablespoons chia seeds
½ teaspoon cinnamon
½ teaspoon nutmeg
1 tablespoon agave syrup

Mix all ingredients in a cup and store in the refrigerator to use regularly. Use as a breakfast spread or on cereal.

Honey chia provides sweetness, taste and texture. It's delicious drizzled over pancakes or quinoa flakes, or simply spread on seeded bread.

Freekeh Granola

1 cup freekeh
2 Granny Smith apples
2 teaspoons vanilla extract
2 teaspoons cinnamon
½ teaspoon sea salt
juice of 2 mandarins or 1 orange
1 tablespoon mandarin zest
juice of ½ lemon
1 tablespoon lemon zest
2 tablespoons chia seeds
½ cup pumpkin seeds
½ cup sunflower seeds
1 cup raisins
1 cup cranberries
maple syrup, to serve

Cook freekeh in 2 cups of water for 35 minutes until soft and set aside.

Add all other ingredients except for the seeds into a food processor and blend until chunky (not pureed). Add to the freekeh.

Add the seeds and store in the refridgerator overnight. Serve with a drizzle of maple syrup.

Freekeh is cracked green wheat, another ancient, delicious and nutritious food. Low in carbohydrates, high in fibre and low-GI, it's low in fat, high in protein, and rich in calcium, iron and zinc. Freekeh does contain gluten, however it is great for bowel health.

Gluten-free Chia Pancakes

Makes 8–10 pancakes

1 cup frozen berries or fresh blueberries

2 tablespoons chia seeds

1 cup organic spelt flour

1 teaspoon nutritional yeast

pinch of salt

1 cup organic rice milk or almond milk

1 cup cashew nuts, soaked 1–2 hours
   and drained

2 ripened bananas

2 tablespoons maple syrup

1 teaspoon virgin coconut oil

Put frozen berries in a small bowl and set aside

Mix half the chia seeds in ½ cup of water, and allow to sit until a gel consistency forms.

Mix flour, yeast, salt and milk together in a large bowl.

Add soaked cashew nuts, bananas, maple syrup and remaining chia seeds to the processor and blend until smooth and creamy. Add to a bowl with other ingredients, slowly mix in and set aside.

Heat coconut oil in a frying pan over high heat and pour in a large ladleful of pancake mixture. Cook until bubbles appear on the surface, (about 2 minutes) and then flip to cook the other side. If you find it difficult to flip the pancake over use two spatulas to help turn over without breaking them apart.

Serve with fresh blueberries or melted frozen berries; drizzle with maple syrup. Try a pancake stack.

These pancakes are gluten and diary free. Nutritional yeast is a deactivated yeast, sold in flakes or as powder. It's a Vitamin B boost you can add to soups and breads.

Coconut oil has many healing benefits and can even help you lose weight. It aids with digestion, and can prevent various stomach and digestion-related problems. It is great for strengthening the immune system.

Seed of Life Bread & Jam

Makes 1 loaf

½ cup chia seeds or seed blend (see Introduction)
1 cup oat flour
1 cup flaxseed meal
1 cup quinoa flour
1 cup spelt flour
1 tablespoon nutritional yeast
½ cup grapeseed oil
½ cup warm water
1 teaspoon sea salt
Raspberry Jam (see next page)

Preheat oven to 60°C/140°F. Mix all ingredients in a food processor or bowl.

Knead well and roll into a log. Place on a lined baking tray and bake for 1 hour.

This seeded bread is best eaten straight from the oven topped with your favorite jam or thyme yoghurt spread (see recipe) Nutritional yeast is a deactivated yeast, sold in flakes or as powder. It's a Vitamin B boost you can add to soups and breads. Quinoa, like the chia seed, is rich in flavour and fibre. It has a low GI, is high in calcium, high in iron and helps deliver oxygen to the brain.

Raspberry Jam

Makes 1 cup

1 cup frozen raspberries
¼ cup pitted dates
¼ cup agave syrup
2 tablespoons chia seeds

Allow raspberries to thaw.

Blend dates, raspberries, agave and chia seeds on a low speed until smooth.

Refrigerate for 24 hours to allow chia seeds to thicken and flavour to infuse. Keep in a glass jar for up to 4 days in the fridge.

One of my basic all-time favourite foods is raspberry jam on grain bread. Now I get more satisfaction out of the wholesome goodness of this jam recipe that the whole family can also enjoy on pancakes, toast or scones.

Quinoa Flakes & Honey Chia

Serves 2

1 cup quinoa flakes
2 tablespoons chia seeds
1 tablespoon goji berries
1 banana, sliced
½ cup almond milk
1 tablespoon Honey Lucia (see recipe in
   this section)

Mix quinoa flakes, chia seeds, goji berries, banana, and almond milk in a bowl and drizzle Honey Lucia over the top.

In winter you can heat the bowl, to add warmth to your food.

Quinoa flakes, nutritious and high in protein, provide a yummy nutty flavour. Eating a wide variety of foods is the key to great health.

Chia Honey Puffs

Serves 1

1 cup puffed millet

1 cup rice milk

1 tablespoon Honey Lucia (see recipe in this section)

1 tablespoon chia seeds

Pour puffed millet in a bowl, add milk and drizzle with Honey Lucia.

Sprinkle with chia seeds on top.

Kids love this healthy version of honey cereal.

Chia Fruit Salad

½ cup fresh blueberries
½ cup strawberries, chopped
½ cup grapes
½ cup mixed seeds: sunflower, sesame,
   pumpkin and chia
1 tablespoon flaxseed oil
½ cup fresh basil leaves, finely chopped
1 teaspoon agave syrup or Honey Lucia
   (see recipe this section)

Wash the fruit ingredients, drain well and add to serving bowl. Sprinkle with seeds and drizzle over flaxseed oil.

Scatter over the basil and sweeten with agave syrup or Honey Lucia.

Tip: Berries are rich in anti-oxidants which protect you from disease and slow the ageing process. All deliver high benefits to strengthen the immune system and boost cognitive function.

A lovely summer fruit salad, with a healthy dose of omega-3 from the chia seeds sprinkled on top.

Chia Puffed Rice

Serves 1

1 cup puffed brown rice

1 cup rice milk

1 tablespoon chia seeds

1 tablespoon mixed seeds: pumpkin,
   sunflower, sesame

1 banana, sliced

1 tablespoon raisins

1 tablespoon flaxseed oil

fresh fruit, chopped, to serve

Place puffed rice in a bowl.

Pour in the milk, chia, mixed seeds, banana and raisins. Drizzle with flaxseed oil.

Serve with chopped fresh fruit. Enjoy with a cup of hot water and lemon.

Low in fat but high in protein and dietary fibre, I eat this often as a snack and it boosts my energy.

Sweet Banana & Blueberry Chia

Serves 2

1 banana, sliced

3 strawberries, sliced

½ cup fresh blueberries

½ grapefruit, peeled and segmented

¼ cup pumpkin seeds

1 tablespoon chia seeds plus extra to serve

1 tablespoon maple syrup

1 tablespoon flaxseed oil

1 teaspoon honey

Place fruit, pumpkin seeds and chia seeds in a bowl.

Drizzle with maple syrup, flaxseed oil and honey.
Sprinkle extra chia seeds on top to serve.

This breakfast or snack is delightfully sweet, the mix of the grapefruit, flaxseed oil and maple syrup along with the texture of the chia seeds gives it a unique and satisfying taste.

Scrambled Tofu & Parsley

Serves 4

300g/10½oz organic tofu
2 teaspoons nutritional yeast
½ teaspoon turmeric
black pepper, to taste
1 teaspoon soy sauce
sea salt
1 tablespoon chia seeds
½ cup fresh parsley, chopped
4 slices of bread, toasted, to serve

Place all ingredients, apart from parsley, in a bowl and mash together with a fork.

Add parsley and serve with toast on the side.

Nutritional yeast is a deactivated yeast, sold in flakes or as powder. It's a Vitamin B boost you can add to soups and breads.

Chia Omelette

Serves 1

2 tablespoons chia seeds
2 tablespoon rice milk
2 eggs
1 tablespoon fresh oregano
salt and pepper
2 tablespoon olive oil
½ tomato, finely chopped
½ cup mushrooms, finely chopped
1 teapoon virgin coconut oil
50g/1¾oz feta or goat's cheese,
   crumbled

Mix chia and rice milk together and set aside for a few minutes for the chia to expand.

Whisk together the eggs, oregano, salt and pepper and olive oil. Add in the chia and milk. Add the tomato and mushrooms.

Heat coconut oil in a frying pan and pour in the egg mixture. Once it starts to look firm on the top, flip to the other side.

Serve with goat's cheese.

Goat's cheese contains less lactose than cow's milk. It's lower in calories, easier to digest and is low in sodium.

Chia Grape & Banana Salad

1 banana, sliced
2 cherry tomatoes, halved
1 cup grapes
1 cup spinach leaves
½ avocado, sliced
1 tablespoon flaxseed oil
1 tablespoon chia seeds
1 tablespoon mixed seeds

Add all ingredients into a shallow bowl. Drizzle flaxseed oil and sprinkle chia and mixed seeds.

Chia seeds by weight are higher in omega-3 than salmon.

Light Meals & Salads

Silverbeet &
Sweet Potato Salad

Serves 2

2 silverbeet leaves, finely chopped
1 teaspoon olive oil
½ small sweet potato
1 teaspoon sea salt
cracked pepper
1 teaspoon garlic, minced
1 cup mixed salad leaves
¼ cup goat's cheese feta
1 tablespoon chia seeds

DRESSING
1 tablespoon olive oil
juice of ½ lemon
1 teaspoon balsamic vinegar
1 tablespoon chia seeds

Coat the silverbeet in a teaspoon of olive oil. Set aside

Fill a saucepan with one cup of water. Add sweet potato, salt, pepper, garlic and bring to the boil. Simmer until water has completely reduced, about 10 minutes.

Place salad leaves, silverbeet and feta in a bowl. Add vegetables and sprinkle with chia seeds.

Mix dressing ingredients together and pour over salad. Toss and enjoy.

Savoury Chia Crepes

Serves 2–4

1 tablespoon chia seeds

1 cup yellow squash, peeled and
chopped

1 tablespoon virgin coconut oil

½ cup flaxseed/linseed meal

½ cup spelt flour

1 teaspoon olive oil

1 teaspoon ground coriander/cilantro
seeds

1 teaspoon cumin powder

juice ½ a lemon

½ tablespoon agave syrup

pinch sea salt

Lemon Mint Yoghurt (see Sauces), to
serve

MARINATED VEGETABLES

1 large field mushroom

½ red/Spanish onion

½ cup cherry tomatoes, quartered

1 tablespoon soy sauce

1 teaspoon olive oil

1 tablespoon apple cider vinegar

Preheat the oven to 100°C/200°F.

First, make the marinated vegetables. Combine mushrooms, onion, tomatoes, soy sauce, olive oil and apple cider vinegar in a large bowl and set aside to marinate for 15–20 minutes.

In a blender or food processor, blend all the ingredients together, except for the marinated vegetables, until the mixture is a smooth paste. Divide into 2–4 crepes and spread mixture onto baking paper and bake on a low heat for 20–30 minutes, until dry and pliable. When cooked, they should peel off the baking paper easily.

When the crepes are cooked, slide them off the paper and place the vegetables in the centre of each and wrap. Serve with Lemon Mint Yoghurt.

Crepes make a great weekend brunch.

Chia Fritatta

Serves 6

2 leeks
coconut oil, for frying
1 teaspoon garlic
1 sweet potato, peeled and cubed
6 sprigs lemon thyme leaves
2 teaspoons virgin coconut oil
6 eggs
½ cup flat-leaf parsley
50g/1¾oz goat's cheese
1 cup wild rocket leaves
coriander/cilantro leaves, to garnish
rocket, to garnish

DRESSING
1 teaspoon chia seeds
2 spring onion/scallions
2 tablespoon flat-leaf parsley
2 tablespoon balsamic
2 tablespoon lemon juice
drop of honey
½ cup olive oil

Process all dressing ingredients. Preheat the oven to 200°C/390°F.

Cut leeks in half and slice thinly. Fry in a pan with coconut oil and garlic until soft.

Cook sweet potato in a pan of water. Add lemon thyme leaves and 1 teaspoon coconut oil. Simmer and allow to cook until softened a little. Drain.

Add 6 eggs to a large bowl, beat well. Add flat-leaf parsley and goat's cheese and whisk together. Add the leeks and sweet potato, stir well.

Pour into a round cake tin or pie dish. Bake in the oven for 20 minutes.

To serve, drizzle over the dressing and garnish with coriander and rocket leaves.

Chickpea & Mint Falafel

Makes 6

2 tablespoons chia seeds

juice of 1 lemon

1 cup chickpeas, canned or presoaked

½ cup quinoa, cooked

1 cup spinach leaves

1 cup mint, packed

½ cup basil leaves

½ cup coriander/cilantro leaves

1 teaspoon cumin seeds

1 teaspoon garlic powder

1 tablespoon olive oil

1 teaspoon sea salt

¼ cup quinoa flakes or oat flour

1 tablespoon virgin coconut oil

fresh kale leaves, to serve

Lemon Mint Yoghurt (see Sauces), to serve

Mix chia seeds and lemon juice together in a glass. Set aside to form a gel.

Blend chickpeas, quinoa, spinach, mint, basil, coriander, cumin, garlic, olive oil and salt in a food processor until the mixture looks crumbly but not too smooth. You want it to have some texture.

Sprinkle quinoa flakes onto a chopping board. Scoop out a tablespoon of the mixture at a time, roll into a ball and roll in the quinoa flakes. Heat coconut oil in a frying pan and cook the falafels for 3–4 minutes on each side or until golden brown.

Serve on a bed of fresh kale leaves with a drizzle of Lemon Mint Yoghurt.

Chia Bruschetta

Serves 2

½ avocado

1 spring onion/scallion, finely chopped

juice of 1 fresh lemon

1 tablespoon chia seeds

2 tablespoons grapeseed oil

1 tomato, chopped

1 cup basil leaves, finely chopped

4 large English spinach leaves, finely chopped

¼ red/Spanish onion, diced

1 tablespoon olive oil

1 teaspoon balsamic vinegar

sea salt

6 slices of Chia & Herb Crispbread (see Breads)

coriander/cilantro leaves, to garnish

Blend avocado, spring onion, lemon, chia seeds and grapeseed oil in a food processor until smooth.

Place tomato, basil leaves, English spinach, Spanish onion and olive oil in a large bowl and toss gently. Drizzle with balsamic vinegar and sprinkle with salt.

Spread the blended avocado on the crisp bread slices. Top with some tomato mixture. Garnish with coriander leaves

A great entrée, snack or meal, topped with plenty of greens and a tasty nutritious spread. Enjoy this on its own or with a side salad.

Avocado & Beetroot Seeded Salad

Serves 2–4

1 cup rocket/arugula leaves, chopped
6 cherry tomatoes, chopped
50g/1¾oz goat's milk feta, crumbled
½ avocado, diced
2 tablespoons raw beetroot, finely sliced
   or grated
1 tablespoon mixed seeds

DRESSING
1 tablespoon chia seeds
¼ teaspoon flaxseed or olive oil
juice of ½ lemon
pinch salt
cracked black pepper

To make the dressing, add the chia seeds, oil, lemon juice, salt and pepper together in a clean, dry jar. Screw on the lid and shake well.

Place the salad ingredients in a large bowl and toss gently. Pour over the dressing and season with salt and cracked pepper.

Brussel Sprout Salad
& Spicy Tomato Sauce

Serves 2–4

1 lettuce, broken up
4 brussel sprouts
1 tomato
1 zucchini/courgette, grated
1 tablespoon chia seeds
Tomato Sauce (See Sauces)

Finely chop all the vegetables. Place all of the chopped vegetables in a large bowl and sprinkle with chia seeds.

Drizzle the salad with fresh tomato sauce.

Brussel sprouts are full of vitamins and minerals – vitamins C, E, A and K. They are also high in omega-3 and the mineral manganese.

Crispbread Sandwich with Avocado & Sprouts

Makes 2 regular or 4 open sandwiches

Chia and Herb Crispbread (see Breads)
Avocado Chia Spread (see Sauces)
Onion Chutney (see Sauces)
1 cup mixed green leaves
1 tomato, sliced
1 cup alfalfa sprouts

First, make the Chia and Herb Crispbread (see recipe).

Once the crispbread is ready, you can assemble the sandwich. Spread two pieces of bread with the avocado spread then onion chutney (if making two regular sandwiches).

Top with mixed leaves, tomato and sprouts. Top with another crispbread, or leave as an open sandwich, depending on the texture of your crisp breads. You may find it easier to eat this with a knife and fork.

'You have the opportunity today to take better care of yourself and live longer.'

Beetroot & Macadamia Feta Cheese Salad

Serves 2

1 cup spinach leaves
½ cups raw beetroot, grated
¼ red/Spanish onion, sliced
6 cherry tomatoes, chopped
1 cup macadamia nuts, ground
juice of 1 lemon squeezed
½ teaspoon nutritional yeast
¼ medium spring onion/scallion, diced
½ teaspoon sea salt
1 tablespoon olive oil
1 tablespoon chia seeds

In a bowl, toss together the spinach leaves, beetroot, onion and cherry tomatoes.

Combine ground macadamia nuts, with half of the lemon juice, nutritional yeast, spring onion and salt. Mix through the salad.

Toss and drizzle with olive oil, chia and remaining lemon juice.

I enjoy beetroot in its simple and natural form. This salad can be enjoyed on its own. Beetroot is your liver's best friend and it is a superfood.

Tip: Beetroot can help detox and cleanse the internal organs, and can help prevent the build up of fatty deposits in the liver. It can help reduce high blood pressure, is packed with nutrients, and is an immune booster.

Enjoy beetroot raw in dips, salads, crispbreads, juices, soups and even cakes.

Spinach Salad with Cashew Nut Dressing

Serves 2

1 cup spinach leaves
6 cherry tomatoes
¼ zucchini/courgette, grated
½ spring onion/scallion, finely sliced

DRESSING
1 teaspoon apple cider vinegar
1 cup raw cashew nuts, soaked
   30 minutes and drained
juice of ½ lemon
1 tablespoon chia seeds
1 teaspoon agave syrup

pinch sea salt

Place spinach, cherry tomatoes, zucchini and spring onion in a large bowl

To make dressing, blend ¼ cup water, apple cider vinegar, drained cashews, lemon juice, chia seeds, agave and salt in a food processor until smooth and creamy.

Pour dressing over salad and lightly massage through with hands.

Quick, healthy and tasty, this salad can be enjoyed with crispbread and dips or simply on its own.

Radish Potato Salad

Serves 3–4

3–4 potatoes, roughly chopped

2 cups Chinese radish, diced

½ cup yellow capsicum/pepper, diced

½ cup green capsicum/pepper, diced

1 tablespoon finely chopped rosemary

2 tablespoons finely chopped green
   olives

½ avocado, diced

½ red/Spanish onion, thinly sliced

1 spring onion/scallion, chopped

CHIA DRESSING

2 tablespoons chia seeds

2 tablespoons tahini

½ tablespoon cumin seeds

juice of 1 lemon

¼ teaspoon soy sauce

1 teaspoon agave

pinch salt

pinch chili powder

2 tablespoons finely chopped parsley, to
   garnish

spring onion/scallion to garnish

Boil the potatoes in a saucepan of hot water until tender when poked with a fork. Drain and set aside.

In a large bowl, add all ingredients except the parsley and the spring onions.

Blend all dressing ingredients in a food processor until smooth. The dressing should be rather thick, but as you mix it through the salad it will become thinner.

When ready to serve, pour dressing over the salad and toss until well combined. Garnish with parsley and spring onions.

Rice Paper Rolls & Sweet Chili Sauce

Serves 2

40g/1½oz dried rice noodles
6 x 16cm diameter rice paper rolls
¼ cup fresh mint leaves
¼ cup fresh coriander/cilantro leaves
1 spring onion/scallion, thinly sliced
1 cucumber, thinly sliced
3 snow peas/mange tout, thinly sliced
1 carrot, peeled thinly sliced
1 long red chili, seeds removed and
  thinly sliced
1 tablespoon chia seeds

CHILI AND LIME DIPPING SAUCE
1 tablespoon chia seeds
¼ cup soy sauce
1 tablespoon agave syrup
juice of 1 fresh lime
½ tablespoon sesame oil
pinch chili flakes

Place noodles in a bowl, cover with boiling water for 5 to 8 minutes or until soft. Drain and set aside.

To soften rice paper rolls, pour warm water into a bowl and dip rice paper in for 30 seconds. Remove from water and place on a clean cloth or board. Place mint leaves, coriander, spring onions, cucumber, snow peas, carrots, chili and a sprinkle of chia seeds in the centre of each rice paper. Fold over and roll ends to enclose filling.

To make dipping sauce, mix all ingredients in a screw top jar and shake until mixed. Serve dipping sauce with rice paper rolls.

One of my favourite light meals, full of clean, fresh and tasty vegetables and a unique dipping sauce. Throw in an extra dose of omega-3 by adding a tablespoon of chia seeds to your dipping sauce, or simply sprinkle them into the salad. This dish leaves you feeling energised, light and satisfied.

Alfredo with Cashew Cream & Macadamia

Serves 2

2 zucchini/courgettes, sliced
6 cherry tomatoes, cut into fours
¼ cup sun-dried tomatoes
½ cup black olives, chopped
1 tablespoon white chia seeds
2 basil leaves, chopped finely
2 spring onion/scallion, chopped finely
olive oil
pinch salt
cracked pepper
Cashew Cream (see Sauces)
Macadamia Crumble (see Sauces)

Halve zucchini lengthwise and slice with vegetable peeler to make long strips of spaghetti.

Add to a large bowl with remaining ingredients.

Add Cashew Cream and mix through. Sprinkle with Macadamia Crumble and serve.

When you eat raw food, you will notice you don't need as much of it, or need to eat the heavier foods you would normally. Lighter food makes you feel lighter and energised. This is one of my favourite recipes, and one I learnt in Bali from head chef Made Ruthna of Fivelements.

Chia Quiche

Serves 4

5 free-range or organic eggs, lightly
  beaten
1 cup self-raising spelt flour
4 cherry tomatoes, quartered
1 zucchini/courgette, grated
½ cup broccoli, finely chopped
½ sweet potato, grated
1 onion, chopped finely
1 teaspoon onion flakes
1 tablespoon chia seeds
1 cup grated cheese, or ½ cup goat's
  milk feta, chopped
pinch sea salt
cracked pepper
spinach leaves to serve

Preheat oven to 160°C/320°F.

Add eggs to a large bowl and whisk together.

Stir in the rest of the ingredients. Add a pinch of salt and cracked pepper and mix well.

Pour into a 20cm/10in flan dish and bake for 30 minutes until cooked and golden brown.

Serve with spinach leaves.

This is a quick and easy dinner we eat at least once a week as a family, it's packed with vegetables.

Soups

Green Soup

Serves 2

2 tablespoons chia seeds
2 cups water
4 cups broccoli
1 cup peas, fresh is best
1 teaspoon garlic powder
1 teaspoon onion powder
1 teaspoon sea salt
1 tablespoon agave syrup
1 tablespoon olive oil
pinch cracked pepper
Herb Crispbreads (see Breads)

Mix chia seeds with 1 cup of water in a bowl, allow to soak until chia seeds form a gel consistency.

Place all other ingredients except olive oil in a saucepan with 1 cup of water and bring to a boil. Simmer for 5 minutes. Allow to cool.

Add olive oil and chia seeds and process until smooth. Serve cold with cracked pepper and Crispbreads.

Chia & Pumpkin Soup

Serves 2

2 tablespoons chia seeds
2 cups water
¼ dense, sweet pumpkin
1 small sweet potato/kumura
1 tablespoon virgin coconut oil
1 tablespoon fresh ginger
pinch of sea salt
Herb Crispbreads (see Breads)
coriander/cilantro leaves, to garnish
cherry tomatoes, to garnish
goat's milk cheese, to garnish

Mix chia seeds with 1 cup of water in a bowl, allow to soak until chia seeds form a gel consistency.

In a saucepan, add the pumpkin, sweet potato, coconut oil, ginger and water. Bring to the boil. Simmer until vegetables are soft. Allow to cool.

Remove the saucepan from the heat and stir in the chia and salt. Using a hand blender, blend the vegetables for 2–3 minutes and return to a gentle heat for about 3 minutes.

Garnish with fresh coriander, cherry tomatoes and goat's cheese. Serve with Herb Crispbread.

Cauliflower Soup

1 garlic clove, finely sliced

1 tablespoon finely diced onion

1 teaspoon grapeseed oil

1 cauliflower, roughly chopped into florets

1 teaspoon fresh oregano

1 teaspoon fresh thyme

1 teaspoon fresh rosemary

black pepper

1 teaspoon ginger

1 teaspoon virgin coconut oil

½ teaspoon tumeric powder

½ teaspoon cumin powder

2 tablespoons chia seeds

1 cup rice milk

In a large pot, sauté garlic and onion in grapeseed oil for about 3–5 minutes until the onion turns soft.

Add the remaining ingredients except for the chia seeds and milk. Cover with water and let the ingredients steam until boiling, then reduce the heat and simmer for 15 minutes or until cauliflower is tender. Set aside for 5 minutes to cool before blending.

Add chia seeds to rice milk and allow to sit for 5 minutes.

Add milk and chia to the pot slowly stirring for 2 minutes until mixed and heated through. Serve.

I like to garnish my soups especially the raw cold soups with raw chopped tomato, spring onion, or cucumber. Drizzle with a little olive oil, sprinkle sea salt and cracked pepper to taste.

Mushroom Soup

Serves 2

½ cauliflower
2 tablespoons chia seeds
2 large field mushrooms
1 teaspoon grapeseed oil
salt
cracked black pepper
coriander/cilantro, cherry tomato and
    goat's cheese to garnish

Break cauliflower into florets, add chia seeds and cover with water. Bring to the boil in a saucepan. Simmer until tender, about 15 minutes. Drain well in a fine-mesh colander.

In a frying pan, sauté the mushrooms in grapeseed oil. Blend cooked cauliflower and mushrooms in a food processor until smooth, adding salt and cracked pepper to taste.

Garnish with coriander, cherry tomato and goat's cheese.

Avocado Soup

Serves 2

1 avocado, pitted
½ green onion/salad onion, chopped
1 tablespoon chia seeds
1 tablespoon olive oil
1 teaspoon sea salt
small pinch chili flakes
cracked black pepper to taste

Place all ingredients in a food processor and add ½ cup water. Blend until smooth and creamy, adding more water if desired. Serve as a cold soup, or warm the bowl and serve with seeded bread or corn chips and use as a dip. If you like, garnish with chopped cherry tomatoes and finely sliced spring onion or cucumber.

Savoury Cauliflower Chia Soup

Serves 2

1 tablespoon chia seeds
½ cup greenwheat freekeh
½ cauliflower
½ zucchini/courgette
2 teaspoons onion flakes
2 teaspoons savoury yeast
1 teaspoon garlic powder
2 teaspoons agave syrup

Mix chia seeds with ½ cup water and set aside to form a gel consistency.

Boil the freekeh in a pot of water for 30 minutes or until soft. Drain and set aside.

In a saucepan, add the cauliflower and zucchini, cover with water and boil until soft. Drain well and add to a food processor.

Add all other ingredients, including freekeh and chia gel, and blend well.

Serve with bread rolls.

Freekeh is an ancient grain processed from wheat that is harvested while the grains are still green. The grains are then roasted. Freekeh contains more protein, vitamins and minerals than wheat. It is high in fibre and low GI.

Roasted Tomato & Fennel Soup with Basil Pesto

Serves 4

VEGETABLE STOCK

1 carrot
1 celery stalk
1 yellow squash
½ onion
3 cups water
sea salt
cracked pepper
1 teaspoon garlic powder
1 teaspoon onion powder

1 large fennel bulb
1 onion, peeled
4 ripe tomatoes
½ garlic bulb
olive oil
sea salt and cracked pepper

PESTO

1 garlic clove
2 tablespoons olive oil
1 handful fresh basil
2 tablespoons pine nuts
1 tablespoon chia seeds

Preheat oven to 180°C/360°F.

To make stock, place all ingredients in a large saucepan of water, cover and bring to the boil. Simmer for 10 minutes, then drain, discard solids and reserve liquid and allow to cool.

Meanwhile, slice fennel and onion, and chop tomato into quarters. Place vegetables and garlic head on an oven tray, drizzle with olive oil and season with sea salt and cracked pepper.

Bake for 40–50 minutes.

Once cooked, remove from oven and allow to cool. Remove garlic skin and place garlic, fennel, onion and tomato in a food processor and blend until smooth. Slowly and carefully add cooled vegetable stock. Blend for 5 minutes or until soup is really smooth.

To make pesto, blend all ingredients in a food processor until chunky.

To serve, pour soup into a bowl, add a tablespoon of pesto and stir through..

Sweet Potato & Coconut Soup

Serves 4

1 tablespoon chia seeds

2 large sweet potatoes, peeled and cut into large chunks

1 onion, finely diced

2 potatoes, peeled and diced

1 tablespoon virgin coconut oil

1 teaspoon sea salt

1 tablespoon nutritional yeast

fresh coriander/cilantro to garnish

cracked pepper to taste

Herb Crispbread to serve (see Breads)

Place chia seeds in a glass bowl, pour over 2 cups water, stir well and set aside to form a gel consistency.

Cover sweet potatoes, onion and potato in a saucepan of water, add coconut oil and salt, and boil until soft.

Remove the potato and set aside to cool for 10 minutes. Place sweet potato and onion in a blender, add chia seeds and yeast and blend well until smooth. Return blended ingredients to the pot and add the potato.

Serve with fresh coriander, cracked pepper to taste and crispbread.

Nutritional yeast is a deactivated yeast, sold in flakes or as powder. It's a Vitamin B boost you can add to soups and breads.

Zucchini Soup

Serves 2

3 zucchinis/courgettes, peeled
juice of 1 lemon
$1/3$ cup olive oil
¼ teaspoon sea salt
1 teaspoon ginger
1 teaspoon onion powder
1 tablespoon agave syrup
1 teaspoon cumin
1 tablespoon chia seeds
2 cups water
cracked pepper, to taste
cherry tomato, spring onion/scallion and
   coriander/cilantro, to serve

Blend all ingredients until smooth.

Garnish with cherry tomato, spring onion and coriander and cracked pepper to taste.

Dips & Sides

Yellow Squash Hummus

Serves 4–6

1 cup walnuts, soaked for 30 minutes

1 tablespoon dried oregano

1 tablespoon dried basil

2 cups yellow pumpkin squash, chopped

2 teaspoons sea salt

1 tablespoon olive oil

1 teaspoon lemon juice

½ spring onion/scallion

1 tablespoon agave syrup

2 teaspoons nutritional yeast

1 tablespoon chia seeds

Process all ingredients until smooth and creamy.

Use as a dip for crispbreads, or as a dressing.

I love a simple and nutritious dip with raw vegetable sticks. Hummus is my favourite, but I do like to use freshly soaked and cooked chickpeas, so it takes a little while. Nutritional yeast is a deactivated yeast, sold in flakes or as powder. It's a Vitamin B boost you can add to soups and breads.

Macadamia Hummus

Serves 4–6

1 cup macadamia nuts, soaked for 20
    minutes
juice of 1 lemon
1 tablespoon chia seeds
1 tablespoon olive oil
1 tablespoon tahini
1 teaspoon garlic powder
½ teaspoon salt
⅓ cup water

Blend all ingredients in a food processor until smooth and creamy.

Use as a dip for crispbreads, or as a dressing.

Classic Hummus

Serves 4–6

1 cup chickpeas, soaked overnight and
    cooked until tender or canned
1 tablespoon chia seeds
1 garlic clove
juice of 1 lemon
2 tablespoons tahini
2 tablespoons olive oil
pinch of sea salt or pink salt

Blend cooked chickpeas with chia, garlic, lemon juice, tahini, olive oil and sea salt until smooth.

Mango & Chia Guacamole

Makes 1 cup

2 avocados, peeled
1 teaspoon salt
1 cup flat-leaf parsley
1 jalapeno chili, deseeded and chopped
2 tablespoons lime or lemon juice
1 tablespoon chia seeds
1 mango, finely chopped

Place all ingredients, except mango, in a food processor and blend well. Garnish with chopped mango.

What I love about this dip is you only need a very small amount to satisfy you. Enjoy along with a green salad, crispbread or raw vegetables.

Salsa Fresca

Makes 1 cup

3 tomatoes, diced
½ cup fresh basil
1 cup flat-leaf parsley
1 cup red/Spanish onion, chopped
1 tablespoon chia seeds
⅓ cup olive oil
juice of 2 lemons
2 teaspoons sea salt

Mix all ingredients together in a large bowl.

Add chopped fresh rocket/arugula for extra flavour if you like. Stir in well.

Serve on its own or with crispbreads or corn chips.

This is best if it sits for an hour but once you add the salt, eat it within four hours, as it can become watery. Serve with hummus and flat bread.

Spicy Salsa

Makes 1 cup

2 red capsicums/peppers, deseeded and
   sliced
½ onion, peeled
3 garlic gloves, peeled
2 tablespoons chia seeds
juice of ½ lime
4 sundried tomatoes
½ cup coriander/cilantro
1 red chili pepper
½ teaspoon salt

Place all ingredients in a food processor and blend until smooth. Keep in a glass jar in the fridge for one week.

Chia Mushrooms

Serves 4

4 large field mushrooms
¼ cup olive oil
¼ cup balsamic vinegar
1 tablespoon chia seeds
sea salt
cracked pepper

Place mushrooms in a large shallow bowl, saturate with oil and balsamic vinegar. Sprinkle over chia seeds, salt and cracked pepper.

Allow to marinate for 1–2 hours. Serve with extra cracked pepper. These mushrooms can be stored for 24 hours and taste even better the next day.

I love to entertain and this is a tasty starter and easy to prepare in advance. After eating these you will always want to enjoy the distinct flavour of a raw marinated mushroom with the subtle texture of chia.

Spicy Chia Cashews

Serves 6

2 cups raw cashews soaked in water for
   1–2 hours and drained
1 tablespoon agave syrup
2 tablespoons maple syrup
1 teaspoon turmeric
1 teaspoon curry powder
pinch chili flakes
1 tablespoon chia seeds
pinch sea salt

Preheat the oven to 150°C/300°F.

Place drained nuts in a bowl and add agave, maple syrup, turmeric, curry powder, chili flakes and salt. Mix until well coated.

Pour the cashews onto a lined baking tray and bake for 10–15 minutes. Remove from the oven and sprinkle with chia seeds.

Add to salads or keep in a clean, glass jar in the fridge.

Keep a batch of these on hand to use in salads or as a snack.

Corn Chips

Serves 4

1 cup ground flaxseeds
2 cups frozen corn, thawed
1 cup water
2 tablespoons olive oil
1 teaspoon cumin seeds
½ red/Spanish onion
½ garlic clove
1 teaspoon sea salt, for sprinkling
1 tablespoon lemon juice
pinch of chili flakes

Preheat oven to 160°C/320°F. Blend all ingredients in a food processor. Spread mixture as finely as possible on baking paper on an oven tray. Use a pizza cutter to create triangle shapes.

Bake on low oven for 40 minutes or until golden crunchy.

Serve with soup or dips.

Cashew Nut Dip

Serves 4

1 cup raw cashews, soaked for
   1–2 hours and drained
1 cup water
1 teaspoon apple cider vinegar
1 teaspoon agave syrup
1 tablespoon chia seeds
pinch of sea salt
juice of ½ lemon

Blend all ingredients in a food processor until smooth and creamy.

Serve with fresh raw vegetable batons.

Onion Dip

1 cup raw cashew nuts soaked 1–2
   hours and drained
1 tablespoon olive oil
1 teaspoon garlic powder
1 teaspoon dried onion flakes
juice of 1 lemon
½ cup water

Blend all ingredients until smooth and creamy.

Pink Milli Dip

Serves 4

1 cup macadamia nuts, soaked for
   2 hours
½ red/Spanish onion
1 tablespoon white chia seeds
juice of 1 lemon
1 tablespoon olive oil
½ cup rice milk
1 teaspoon pink salt

Place all ingredients in a food processor and blend until smooth. It may take 5 minutes until smooth and creamy.

My kids love this fresh, light and healthy snack, served as a spread on rice cakes, with avocado and garnished with tomato. Or use as a quick and easy sauce for pasta, with cherry tomatoes.

Breads

Chia & Herb Crispbread

Serves 4

1 cup basil

sea salt

1 cup organic wholemeal flour

1 tablespoon mixed seeds (sesame, sunflower, pumpkin, linseed/flaxseed)

1 tablespoon chia seeds

2 tablespoons grapeseed oil

2 tablespoons cooked quinoa

½ cup warm water

Preheat oven to 160°C/325°F.

In a food processor or blender, blend basil, salt, flour, seeds and chia. Pour the mixture into a bowl and add the oil, quinoa and water. Mix everything together.

Place ingredients on a chopping board and knead and roll into a ball. Thinly roll out on baking paper and bake until golden brown. Break into square pieces. Serve with soup or dips.

A quick and easy snack to be enjoyed with your favourite dips.

Chia Seed & Flaxseed Rolls

Makes 6–8

¼ cup freekeh
1 cup oat flour
1 cup spelt flour
1 cup flaxseed/linseed meal
½ cup LSA
½ cup chia seeds
½ cup nutritional yeast
1 teaspoon salt
½ cup raisins or goji berries
50ml/1¾fl oz olive oil
½ cup warm water

Preheat oven to 150°C/300°F.

Boil the freekeh in a saucepan of water until soft. Drain and set aside.

Place all dry ingredients in a bowl, including dried fruit, and mix. Stir in the freekeh then add the olive oil and water. Knead well to make a soft dough, adding more water if necessary.

Shape into small rolls on baking paper or spoon into a muffin tray.

Bake for 30–45 minutes until crispy.

Nutritional yeast is a deactivated yeast, sold in flakes or as powder. It's a Vitamin B boost you can add to soups and breads.

Gluten-free Chia Seed Rolls

Serves 12

2 tablespoons chia seeds
½ cup boiling water
½ cup flaxseed meal
1½ teaspoon nutritional yeast
1 tablespoon agave syrup
2 tablespoons olive oil
1 cup water
½ cup oat flour
½ cup almond meal
½ cup spelt flour
2 tablespoons psyllium husks
pinch sea salt
1 teaspoon apple cider vinegar

Preheat oven to 200°C/400°F.

Mix chia seeds with boiling water and add flax meal.

In a large bowl, combine the nutritional yeast, agave syrup, olive oil and 1 cup of water together. Add in the flours, almon meal, psyllium husks, salt and cider vinegar and combine. Slowly mix in the chia mixture and stir everything together.

Transfer the mixture to a chopping board and knead well. Transfer to a plate, cover with plastic wrap and place in the refrigerator for 30 minutes.

Remove from refrigerator and spoon mixture into cupcake patties lined into a 12-hole muffin tin.

Bake in the oven for 40 minutes or until golden.

Trying to create gluten-free bread without the gums and Xanthan, which mix with water and swell, can be a challenge, so I replace it with chia and water, which also mixes with water and swells. Nutritional yeast is a deactivated yeast, sold in flakes or as powder. It's a Vitamin B boost you can add to soups and breads.

Herb Crackers

Serves 4

1 cup quinoa flour
1 cup almond meal
1 cup LSA or flaxseed/linseed meal
1 tablespoon chia seeds
2 teaspoons salt
2 tablespoons nutritional yeast
1 tablespoon fresh oregano
1 tablespoon fresh thyme
1 teaspoon garlic powder
1 teaspoon onion powder
2 tablespoons olive oil
2 cups water

Preheat oven to 180°C/360°F.

In a large bowl, mix dry ingredients and fresh herbs, then slowly mix in oil and water. Form into a dough and press out onto baking paper.

Bake for 20–30 minutes, or until crispy. Be careful not to burn.

Serve with dips (see Sauces and Dips).

Nutritional yeast is a deactivated yeast, sold in flakes or as powder. It's a Vitamin B boost you can add to soups and breads.

Barbecue Crisps

1 cup oat flour
1 cup quinoa flour
1 cup LSA meal
2 tablespoons psyllium husks
2 tablespoons nutritional yeast
2 tablespoons olive oil
2 teaspoons sea salt
2 tablespoons maple syrup
1 tablespoon chili flakes
1 cup Barbecue Sauce (see Sauces)
½ cup or water
1 tablespoon chia seeds

Preheat oven to 180°C/360°F. Mix dry ingredients in a large bowl, slowly mix in oil, maple syrup water. Form dough, and press out onto baking paper, bake for 20–30 minutes, or until crispy. Be careful not to burn.

Serve with dips (see Sauces and Dips).

Nutritional yeast is a deactivated yeast, sold in flakes or as powder. It's a Vitamin B boost you can add to soups and breads.

Seeded Nutty Bread

Makes 1 loaf

1 cup LSA

2 cups quinoa flour

1 cup spelt flour

½ cup self-raising/bakers gluten-free
   flour

1 tablespoon nutritional yeast

1 cup mixed seeds

½ cup olive oil

pinch of salt

1 cup warm water

4 fresh dates, chopped

Preheat oven to 60°C/140°F. Mix all ingredients, except for the dates, in a food processor or bowl. Add more water if needed to form a dough consistency.

Add the chopped dates. Knead well and roll into a log.

Place on a baking tray and bake in the oven for 1 hour.

Nutritional yeast is a deactivated yeast, sold in flakes or as powder. It's a Vitamin B boost you can add to soups and breads.

Mains

Thai Chia Curried Salad

Serves 4

4 cups mixed salad leaves
½ cup sundried tomatoes, finely chopped
1 avocado, sliced
½ red capsicum/pepper, chopped
½ yellow capsicum/pepper, chopped
½ green capsicum/pepper, chopped
1 tablespoon chia seeds
1 spring onion/scallion, finely chopped
1 tablespoon dessicated or sliced
   coconut
½ cup flat-leaf parsley
½ cup Spicy Chia Cashews (see Dips and
   Sides)
pinch sea salt
cracked pepper, to taste
½ cup Thai Chia Dressing (see Sauces
   and Dressings)
handful corianer/cilantro leaves, to
   garnish

Place salad leaves in a large salad bowl. Add sundried tomatoes, avocado and peppers. Sprinkle over chia seeds. Top with spring onions, coconut, flat-leaf parsley and spicy cashews.

Add the salt and pepper, Thai chia dressing and toss gently. Garnish with coriander.

I have many memories of eating Thai food with my girls, and I enjoyed creating this recipe knowing everything is clean and wholesome. This salad will leave a sensational taste on your palate and take you back for more.

Chia Vegan Tacos

Serves 4

TACO FILLING
1 cup walnuts
1 tablespoon tamari
1 tablespoon chia seeds
1 teaspoon olive oil
1 teaspoon cumin
¼ teaspoon ground pepper
¼ teaspoon ground coriander/cilantro
¼ teaspoon chili powder

TOMATO SALSA
2 tomatoes, diced
1 green chili, finely diced
1 red/Spanish onion, finely diced
1 cup coriander/cilantro
juice of 1 lemon

6 large cos lettuce leaves

1 avocado, diced
Chia Sour Cream (see Sauces)
Salsa Fresca (see Dips and Sides)
coriander/cilantro, to garnish

Process all the filling ingredients in a food processor, until small crumbs form and it looks a little like minced meat.

Make the tomato salsa, by mixing together the tomatoes, chili, onion and coriander. Season with the lemon juice and salt.

In one bowl, place the avocado. In another bowl, place the Chia Sour Cream and in another the Salsa Fresca.

To assemble tacos, use the lettuce leaves as the shell. Place the filling on the bottom, add some tomato salsa then top with avocado, Salsa Fresca and Sour Cream. Garnish with coriander.

These healthy tacos may not be like the traditional tacos you are used to but will leave you feeling satisfied and energised.

Macaroni Chia

4 yellow pumpkin squash, peeled

2 tablespoons chia seeds

1 cup raw cashew nuts, soaked for
  2 hours and drained

¼ cup olive oil

½ teaspoon sea salt

¼ cup nutritional yeast (see
  Introduction)

1 teaspoon onion flakes

2 tablespoons lemon juice

¼ spring onion/scallion, finley sliced

pinch of turmeric

½ garlic clove, mashed

pinch of paprika

½ cup walnuts

pinch chili flakes

sea salt, extra, to taste

Slice squash with a vegetable peeler or slicer to create long noodles and allow to sit.

Mix 1 tablespoon of chia seeds with all other ingredients, except pumpkin noodles, walnuts, chili flakes and extra sea salt. Process until smooth and creamy. Add to yellow squash and massage through with your hands slowly and gently, until thoroughly mixed.

Process walnuts, remaining chia seeds and a pinch of chili flakes and sea salt together. Top squash mixture with walnut crumbs.

Nutritional yeast is a deactivated yeast, sold in flakes or as powder. It's a Vitamin B boost you can add to soups and breads. My girls love this dish.

Chia Seafood Salad

Serves 2

1 spring onion/scallion, finely chopped
1 cup fresh coriander/cilantro
½ cup flat-leaf parsley
1 teaspoon chia seeds
½ garlic clove
¼ yellow chili, deseeded and chopped
1 teaspoon virgin coconut oil
juice of ½ lemon
12 raw shrimp/prawns, peeled and
   deveined
fresh spinach leaves
½ cup Thai Chia Dressing (see Sauces
   and Dressings)

In a bowl, combine spring onion, coriander, parsley and chia and set aside.

Sauté the garlic and chili in coconut oil. Add prawns over a high heat with lemon juice until they change colour.

Line a bowl with fresh spinach. Toss prawns in spring onion and parsley and spoon the prawns on top of the spinach. Drizzle with Thai Chia Dressing.

Crusted Fish 'n' Chia

Serves 4

2 large fish fillets
2 tablespoons olive oil
juice of ½ lemon
pinch of sea salt
2 tablespoons chia seeds
2 tablespoons LSA
1 tablespoon onion flakes
1 teaspoon virgin coconut oil
Barbecue Sauce (see next page)
lemon wedges, to serve
Chips (see next page)

Cut the fish into 2–3 in/5–7 cm pieces

Pour oil into a small bowl, add lemon and a pinch salt.

In another bowl, mix chia seeds, LSA and onion flakes.

Dip the fish pieces in the oil, then dip into the seed mixture and place on a large plate. Once all fish pieces are crusted, place the plate in the fridge for 30 minutes.

Heat the coconut oil in a pan. Cook fish for 10 minutes each side.

Serve with Barbecue Sauce on the side, lemon wedges and chips.

Fish and chips on a picnic rug bedside the seaside is a fond memory I hold of when the girls were toddlers. These days I get to enjoy a healthier version which melts in your mouth and satisfies your palate.

Barbecue Sauce

Makes 1 cup

1 cup sundried tomatoes

$^1/_3$ cup maple syrup

¼ cup apple cider vinegar

1 spring onion/scallion peeled and chopped

1 garlic clove

1 tablespoon fresh chili, deseeded and chopped

1 teaspoon chili powder

1 teaspoon soy sauce (I use unpasteurised soy sauce)

1 tablespoon chia seeds

Soak sundried tomatoes for 1–2 hours in 1 cup of water, reserving ½ cup of soaking water.

In a food processor, blend all ingredients with the soaking water until smooth. Store in refrigerator for a week.

Chips

Serves 4

4 large organic potatoes, peeled and cut
  into long narrow wedges
1 tablespoon virgin coconut oil
1 sprig rosemary
sea salt
1 tablespoon chia seeds

Preheat oven to 150°C/300°F.

Steam potatoes over a pot of boiling water for
10 minutes.

Add potatoes to a baking dish, drizzle with coconut oil,
sprinkle with rosemary and sea salt.

Bake slowly for 15–20 minutes until golden brown, and
sprinkle with chia.

Crusty Chia Salmon

Serves 4

CRUSTY TOPPING

1 tablespoon chia seeds
1 teaspoon mustard seeds
1 tablespoon chopped fresh dill
2 tablespoons chopped fresh parsley
1 garlic clove
zest of 1 lemon
3 tablespoons lemon juice
1 spring onion/scallion, sliced
1 tablespoon olive oil
½ cup quinoa flakes
sea salt and cracked pepper to taste
½ cup mixed seeds

4 small salmon fillets
baby spinach, to serve
lemon wedges, to serve

Preheat oven to 180°C/360°F. Line a baking tray with baking paper.

Blend all the crusty topping ingredients until chunky, being careful not to make the mixture too smooth.

Spread mixture over one side of the salmon pieces and bake for 15–20 minutes until the topping is golden and crusty.

Serve on a bed of baby spinach with lemon wedges.

Chia Fish Cakes

1 sweet potato, peeled

1 cup cauliflower, trimmed and cut into florets

200g/7oz firm, white fish fillets, such as ling

1 red chili, deseeded and finely chopped

½ teaspoon lemon zest

juice of 1 lemon

2 tablespoons chia seed

3 spring onions/scallions, finely sliced

½ cup fresh coriander/cilantro, chopped

1 tablespoon virgin coconut oil

½ cup Tomato Sauce (see Sauces)

½ cup Thai Chia Dressing (see Sauces)

Dice the sweet potato into quarters and gently boil for 20 minutes until they are soft.

Steam the cauliflower for 10 minutes until it is tender.

Mash the sweet potatoes and add them to a large bowl.

Place cauliflower in a food processor with the fish, chili, lemon zest and juice and process until the mixture is well combined but retains texture.

Add to the bowl with the mashed sweet potatoes and mix in chia seeds, spring onions and coriander until well combined.

Using your hands form small patties approximately 2in/6cm in diameter.

Heat a non-stick frying pan with a little coconut oil and cook fish cakes for 3–4 minutes on each side.

Place on an oven tray lined with baking paper in a low oven to keep warm until ready to serve. Serve with a green salad and Tomato Sauce or Thia Chia Dressing.

Tomato Chia Pasta Squash

Serves 6

MACADAMIA RICOTTA

1 cup raw macadamia nuts, soaked 1–2 hours

juice of 1 lemon

¼ cup olive oil

½ tablespoon nutritional yeast (see Introduction)

1 tablespoon white chia seeds

½ spring onion/scallion

½ teaspoon sea salt

MINT BASIL PESTO

1 cup fresh basil

½ cup fresh mint leaves

½ cup pistachio nuts

2 tablespoons olive oil

1 tablespoon chia seeds

½ teaspoon salt

pinch cracked black pepper

TOMATO GINGER CHIA SAUCE

½ cup sundried tomato, diced

1 tomato, diced

1 spring onion/scallion, chopped

juice of 1 lemon

¼ cup oil

1 teaspoon agave syrup

½ teaspoon salt

¼ cup hot water with tablespoon ginger

small pinch chili flakes

6–8 yellow squash

olive oil

2 tablespoons chia seeds

cracked pepper

fresh basil leaves, to garnish

fresh rocket/arugula leaves, to garnish (optional)

Process all macadamia ricotta ingredients until smooth and set aside. Blend all Pesto ingredients well and set aside. Blend all tomato ginger chia sauce ingredients and set aside.

Slice ends of squash and cut into 4in/12cm pieces. Create pasta pieces by slicing each piece thinly and diagonally with a sharp knife. Lay squash in the bottom of a large oval shallow dish and drizzle with olive oil. Sprinkle with chia seeds, and add a layer of macadamia ricotta (approximately one third of the quantity made) then a layer of yellow squash. Spread over tomato sauce, then macadamia ricotta, then pesto and then tomato sauce. Repeat layers, topping with fresh basil and rocket.

This dish is creamy and rich and just as satisfying as an Italian pasta dish...the only difference is there is no heavy pasta! It is fun to make and the whole family will enjoy it.

Spicy Eggplant Rolls with Rosemary Mash

Serves 4

½ large eggplant/aubergine thinly sliced
   lengthwise
1 tablespoon sea salt

MARINADE
½ tablespoon sea salt
½ dried Thai chili
¼ cup water
1 tablespoon maple syrup
2 tablespoons olive oil
1 tablespoon soy sauce
1 tablespoon apple cider vinegar
pinch of chili flakes
¼ teaspoon cumin seeds
1 tablespoon chia seeds
pinch black pepper

ROSEMARY MASH
2 cups cauliflower, chopped
1 cup raw cashew nuts, soaked 1–2
   hours, drained
2 teaspoons dried rosemary
1 tablespoon fresh rosemary
1 tablespoon chia seeds
2 teaspoons garlic powder
1 teaspoon nutritional yeast (optional,
   see Introduction)

Place eggplant and salt in a bowl, toss well and allow to sit for 1–2 hours.

Blend all marinade ingredients and place in a small bowl.

Preheat oven to 180°C/360°F.

Squeeze any liquid from eggplant and add slices to the marinade. Allow to marinate for 30 minutes.

To make the rosemary mash, cook the cauliflower in boiling water until soft. Drain and put the cauliflower into a food processor and blend until smooth. Add in the remaining mash ingredients and blend well until fluffy and creamy.

Roll the mash inside each of the eggplant slices and use skewers to hold them together. On a lined baking tray, bake for 15–20 minutes or until soft and golden.

Mum's Chia Casserole

Serves 4

2 tablespoons chia seeds

1 tablespoon virgin coconut oil, or butter

1 onion, diced

500g (1½lb) blade, chuck or gravy beef steak, cubed

2 carrots, diced

1 cup red quinoa, cooked

2 tablespoons spelt flour, or gluten free flour

2 tablespoons honey

1 tablespoon hot curry powder (Madras)

2½ teaspoons mustard

½ teaspoon salt and pepper, to taste

Mix ½ cup water with chia. Stir well and allow to sit for a few minutes to form a gel consistency.

In a saucepan over a medium-high heat, melt coconut oil and sauté onion until soft.

Place onion in the base of a casserole dish and put the meat on top. Add the carrots and quinoa.

Mix flour, honey, chia gel, curry powder and mustard together to form a paste. Add ½ cup water and mix well. Pour over steak. Cover the dish, season and bring to boil. Simmer and cook slowly on the stove top on a low heat for 2½ hours.

My Dad is a big lover of premium meat and often had a freezer full of lamb and beef. Dad loves throwing a casserole together and his tip is to always cook it slowly so the meat is tender and melts in your mouth. This recipe is for the whole family.

Chicken Chia Schnitzel

2 chicken breasts, halved
2 tablespoons chia seeds
½ cup water
juice of 1 lemon
1 cup quinoa flakes
2 tablespoons basil leaves, finely
    chopped
2 tablespoons chives, finely chopped
½ cup oat flour
virgin coconut oil for trying
lemon wedges to serve

Gently place chicken breasts between plastic wrap, and pound with a mallet to flatten.

Mix chia, water and lemon in a cup. Stir well and set aside and allow to form a gel consistency.

Combine quinoa flakes and herbs in a shallow dish.

Scatter oat flour on a plate and pour chia into a shallow bowl.

Coat each chicken piece in flour, then dip into the chia and then roll well in the quinoa flakes.

In a saucepan, heat the coconut oil and fry each piece of crumbed chicken for 5 minutes each side or until well cooked and golden.

Drain on kitchen paper. Serve with baked sweet potato and potato chips with rosemary and a side of steamed vegetables. Serve with lemon wedges.

For chicken nuggets, cut the breast pieces into cubes. Coconut oil has many health benefits and contains lauric acid, a 'miracle' compound because of its unique health promoting properties. Choose virgin coconut oil and avoid the transfats that can be introduced in the refining process.

Tomato Basil Pizza

Serves 4

CRUST

1 cup flaxseed/linseed meal
1 tablespoon dried oregano
1 tablespoon dried basil
1 tablespoon dried mixed herbs
2 tablespoon chia seeds
2 cups yellow pumpkin squash, chopped
1 cup walnuts, soaked 1 hour
2 teaspoons sea salt
2 tablespoons olive oil
1 tablespoon lemon juice
½ spring onion/scallion, finely diced
2 teaspoons nutritional yeast (see Introduction)
1 teaspoon agave syrup

TOMATO SAUCE

1 cup tomatoes
1 cup sundried tomatoes soaked for 20 minutes
¼ teaspoon dried basil
pinch of sea salt
1 teaspoon agave syrup
1 teaspoon oregano
1 tablespoon chia seeds

TOPPING

1 tablespoon chia seeds
1 cup macadamia nuts, soaked 1 hour
¾ teaspoon lemon zest
juice of ¼ lemon
¼ spring onion/scallion
¼ garlic clove
pinch of sea salt and cayenne
fresh basil to garnish

Preheat oven to 120°C/240°F. To make the crust, place flaxseed meal, dried herbs and chia seeds in a bowl and set aside. Process remaining ingredients until smooth, and add to flaxseed meal mixture. Stir well. Using crust mixture, press out four pizza bases out onto baking paper and bake in oven until completely dry, about 10 minutes.

Make the tomato sauce by blending all ingredients together until smooth. Set aside.

Make the topping by mixing the chia seeds with 1 cup of water and set aside until it forms a gel consistency. Place the rest of the topping ingredients, except the basil, in a blender and process until smooth.

To make pizza, spread pizza bases with tomato sauce, then add topping and garnish with fresh basil leaves.

Chia Bolognese

Serves 2–4

2 tablespoons chia seeds
juice of ½ lemon
2 tablespoons tamari sauce
pinch sea salt
2 garlic cloves, chopped
100g/3½oz walnuts, coarsely ground
2 spring onions/scallions, chopped finely
1 carrot, diced
1 red pepper/capsicum, chopped
1 tomato, diced
2 tablespoon tomato paste
250g/9oz minced meat (optional)
spaghetti pasta for 2
2 tablespoons parmesan cheese or to
    taste

In a bowl, add chia, lemon juice, tamari and salt together and mix well.

In a small frying pan, sauté garlic lightly in some coconut oil over a medium heat.

In a food processor, blend the chia mixture with ground walnuts and sautéed garlic until it forms a crumble mixture. Add spring onion, carrot and pepper. Add the fresh tomato and tomato paste.

If you are using meat, sauté the meat in olive oil until it is browned and cooked through and add to the chia mixture.

In a large saucepan, boil the spaghetti pasta until al dente. Drain and return to the heat. Combine pasta and bolognese sauce together in a large pan and cooked well through or to your taste.

Serve with parmesan cheese.

Quick Family Chia Pizza

Serves 4

BASE
2 cups gluten-free flour
1 sachet dried yeast
sea salt
1 generous tablespoon olive oil
1 tablespoon honey

TOPPING
Tomato Sauce
  (see Tomato Basil Pizza recipe)
goat's cheese, chunks
red and/or green capsicum/pepper, finely
  sliced
mushrooms, finely sliced
rocket/arugula leaves, chopped
spring onion/scallion, diced
fresh tomato slices
avocado slices
sea salt
1 tablespoon chia seeds

Preheat oven to 200°C/400°F.

To make the base, mix the dry ingredients together. Add oil, honey and ½ cup of hot water. Knead until it forms a nice dough, then wrap with plastic wrap and place in fridge for 30 minutes until it rises and swells.

Take out and roll, it should feel light and fluffy.

Roll out 4 thin bases onto baking paper. Bake in the oven for 20–25 minutes or until crispy and golden. Remove from the oven. Spread with Tomato Sauce and then add the toppings of your choice or let the kids choose their own. The pizza doesn't need baking again, it's ready to eat!

For Hawaiian Pizza, use tomato sauce and add mozzarella cheese, pineapple and ham for the topping.

Shepherd's Pie

Serves 4

½ cup lentils, cooked
½ cup cooked quinoa
1 large onion, chopped finely
1 tablespoon virgin coconut oil
3 garlic cloves, crushed
1 can tomatoes
1 tablespoon mixed herbs
2 tablespoon chia seeds
1 tablespoon tomato paste
1 tablespoon Barbecue Sauce (see
    Sauces)
1 tablespoon Tomato Sauce (see Sauces)
500g/17½oz minced meat (optional)
½ cup peas, cooked

TOPPING
4 potatoes or sweet potatoes, peeled and
    diced
40g/1½oz butter
½ cup rice milk
2 tablespoon chia seeds

2 tablespoons goat's cheese
2 tablespoons quinoa flakes
chutney

In a large frying pan, heat the coconut oil over a medium-high heat and sauté the onion until golden. Add garlic, tomatoes, herbs, chia seeds, tomato paste and sauces and cook for a few minutes. Add the lentils, quinoa, salt and pepper and stir well.

If you are using meat, sauté the meat in a separate pan for 15 minutes until browned and cooked. Add to the lentil mix.

Bring the mixture to the boil and simmer for 5 minutes. Cool and use a masher or stick blender to process until smooth. Stir in the cooked peas

Preheat the oven to 200°C/400°F.

Place the potatoes in a large saucepan and cover with water. Boil the potatoes until tender. Drain and return to the saucepan. Add in the butter and rice milk and mash well with a potato masher. Add chia seeds and continue mashing until smooth. Season with salt and pepper.

Spoon the lentil quinoa mixture into a 2-litre ovenproof baking dish. Use a fork to spread mash on the top. Top with crumbled goat's cheese mixed with quinoa flakes. Bake until golden brown, approximately 20 minutes. Serve with chutney.

Chia Quinoa Lasagne

Serves 4

500g/17½oz pumpkin, peeled,
  cut into 1cm (½in) slices
1½ tablespoons olive oil
2 cups rice milk
2 tablespoons chia seeds
1 cup quinoa, cooked
1 medium brown onion, finely
  chopped
2 garlic cloves, crushed
1 medium capsicum/red pepper,
  chopped
2 medium zucchini/courgette,
  halved and sliced
1 carrot, diced
200g/7oz button mushrooms,
  thickly sliced
400g/14oz can diced tomatoes,
  with oregano and basil
80g/2½oz baby spinach
30g/1oz virgin coconut oil
2 tablespoons spelt flour
1 cup reduced-fat grated
  mozzarella cheese (optional)
125g/4oz dried lasagna pasta
  sheets

Preheat the oven to 180°C/350°F. Arrange pumpkin, in a single layer, on a lined baking tray. Drizzle with 2 teaspoons oil. Bake for 20 minutes or until tender. Set aside.

Mix rice milk and chia seeds together and set aside to form a gel consistency.

Heat remaining oil in a heavy-based frying pan over medium heat. Cook the onion, garlic, capsicum, zucchini, carrot and mushrooms, stirring, for 10 minutes or until carrot is tender. Stir in tomatoes. Bring to the boil then reduce heat to low. Simmer for 10 minutes or until sauce has thickened. Remove from heat. Stir in spinach. Cover and set aside for 2 minutes or until spinach has wilted. Season with salt and pepper.

Heat coconut oil in a saucepan over medium heat until foaming. Add flour. Cook, stirring for 1 minute or until bubbling. Remove from heat. Add chia gel gradually, stirring to prevent lumps forming. Return pan to heat. Cook, stirring, for 5 minutes or until sauce boils and thickens. Remove pan from heat. Stir in half the cheese. Set aside.

Lightly grease a 25cm/10in square baking dish. Spoon half the tomato mixture into the dish, then half of the pumpkin, then half of the lasagna sheets, breaking sheets to fit. Add chia mixture on top of lasagne. Repeat layers, finishing with the chia mixture. Sprinkle with remaining cheese. Bake for 40 minutes or until golden.

Chia Lamb Cutlets

Serves 2–3

6 lamb cutlets
1 cup quinoa flakes
1 cup flat-leaf parsley, finely chopped
2 sprigs rosemary leaves, chopped
1 teaspoon parmesan cheese, grated
pinch sea salt
2 tablespoons chia seeds
½ cup spelt flour
1 egg
2 tablespoons virgin coconut oil, for
  frying

Flatten cutlets with a mallet.

Combine quinoa, parsley, rosemary, parmesan, salt and chia. Place in a bowl.

Place flour on a plate.

Whisk egg in a shallow bowl.

Coat each cutlet with flour, shaking off excess, then dip into egg, then chia quinoa mix.

Heat oil in a frying pan on a high heat. Cook each cutlet for 3 minutes on each side slowly and until golden brown.

Do you ever get a late-afternoon energy slump? Adding chia to your food or drinks will turn your body into an energy powerhouse so you'll feel a steady energy burn all day, rather than ups and downs that will have you reaching for the nearest sugary quick fix.

Chia Tuna Bake

Serves 4

2 cups sweet potato, cubed

2 tablespoon chia seeds

1 cup rice milk

2 tablespoons virgin coconut oil

2 tablespoons spelt flour

salt and pepper to taste

40g/1½oz goat's cheese plus extra if required

1 tablespoon wholegrain mustard seeds

400g/14oz tin tuna

½ cup peas

½ cup quinoa flakes

1 tablespoon chia seeds

1 cup fresh rosemary leaves

Bring a pot of water to the boil and cook sweet potato until soft. Drain.

Mix chia seeds and rice milk together, stir well and allow to sit for 5 minutes.

Warm coconut oil in a pan and add flour, stirring for 1 minute. Add chia gel, salt and pepper to taste, whisking continually until there are no lumps. Bring to the boil, reduce heat and simmer until it is smooth and creamy.

Preheat oven to 200°C/400°F.

Stir in the sweet potato, goat's cheese and mustard seeds. Add the tuna and peas and pour mixture into an ovenproof dish.

Combine quinoa, chia seeds and rosemary leaves to make a crumble. Sprinkle over the top and add extra cheese and black pepper.

Bake for 20 minutes until golden brown.

Chia Mushroom Frittata

Serves 2

2 tablespoons chia seeds
1 cup rice milk
3 spring onions/scallions
2 tablespoons virgin coconut oil
2 cups mushrooms, chopped
1 garlic clove, crushed
½ onion, finely chopped
½ cup corn kernels
1 cup flat-leaf parsley
1 cup quinoa, cooked
6 eggs
½ cup spelt flour
1 teaspoon baking powder
40g/1½oz goat's cheese
salt and pepper

Mix chia and rice milk together. Stir well and set aside to form a gel consistency.

In a frying pan, sauté spring onions in coconut oil. Add mushrooms, garlic, onion, corn and parsley and sauté for 5 minutes. Add cooked quinoa, and cook for a further minute.

Whisk 6 eggs well, add to a large bowl with the chia gel. Sift the flour and baking powder and stir into the egg mixture. Fold in goat's cheese, salt and pepper.

Place the mixture into a baking dish and bake for 45 minutes or until golden brown.

Couscous & Chia Basil

Serves 2

1 cup couscous
1 tablespoon chia
1 cup boiling water
pinch sea salt
1 tablespoon olive oil
1 garlic clove, crushed
1 tablespoon virgin coconut oil
1 spring onion/scallion, finely chopped
½ cup sundried tomatoes
2 cups fresh tomato, finely chopped
1 cup basil leaves

DRESSING
2 tablespoons balsamic vinegar
1 lemon
2 tablespoons olive oil
1 tablespoon chia seeds

Add couscous, chia and boiling water to a large bowl. Add salt and olive oil, stir, cover and sit for 10 minutes.

Sauté garlic in coconut oil. Add spring onion, sundried tomatoes, fresh tomato and basil for 3 minutes.

Combine all ingredients into a bowl.

Add dressing ingredients in a glass jar and shake well.

Drizzle dressing over the couscous. Serve on its own or a bed of rocket.

Chia Mushroom Burgers

Serves 2–4

2 tablespoons chia seeds
2 tablespoons olive oil
1 tablespoon soy sauce
2 tablespoons plum sauce
1 tablespoon apple cider vinegar
3 cups chopped field mushrooms
1 cup eggplant/aubergine, chopped
1 cup almonds, soaked for 1–2 hours
½ cup pumpkin seeds, soaked 1–2 hours
¼ cup sunflower seeds
½ tablespoon coriander/cilantro
1 spring onion/scallion, chopped
½ garlic clove
1 cup parsley, chopped
sea salt
cracked pepper

Place chia seeds, olive oil, soy sauce, plum sauce, and apple cider vinegar in a bowl and stir well. Toss in mushrooms and eggplant, set aside to marinate for 20–30 minutes.

Process almonds, pumpkin seeds, sunflower seeds and coriander in a food processor into small pieces, being careful not to over-blend. Place mixture in a large bowl.

Preheat oven to 150°C/300°F. In a food processor, blend marinated mushrooms and eggplant with spring onion, garlic, and parsley until chunky, then add to bowl with seed mixture. Stir well, and season with salt and cracked pepper.

Squeeze handfuls into round patties and place carefully on a baking tray. Use a spatula to flatten burgers. You can eat these raw, but they are better dehydrated or baked slowly until a crust is formed.

Roast Chicken with Chia Stuffing

Serves 4

STUFFING

2 cups sourdough crusty bread

1 cup mixed fresh herbs—mint, parsley, oregano, rosemary

2 tablespoons chia seeds plus ½ cup water mixed to form a gel consistency

1 medium-sized chicken

1 garlic clove

2 tablespoons virgin coconut oil

1 tablespoon honey

4 large potatoes

pinch salt

cracked pepper

Preheat oven to 160°C/325°F.

Process sourdough bread until it forms crumbs. Add fresh mixed herbs and mix well. Transfer to a bowl and fold in the water and chia seeds, mix well. Stuff the chicken.

Place chicken in a large baking dish. Cut garlic into 2–3 slices, pierce the chicken 2–3 times with a knife and insert the garlic cloves. Brush chicken with coconut oil and honey

Cut potatoes into cubes, and place around the chicken. Season with salt and pepper and sprinkle with fresh rosemary.

Bake slowly for two hours.

Vegetarian Pies

PASTRY

2 cups quinoa flour, or wholemeal spelt
   flour
½ teaspoon salt
1 teaspoon baking powder
125g/4oz cold butter
½ cup cold water

FILLING

½ cup lentils, cooked
½ cup quinoa, cooked
1 large onion, chopped finely
1 tablespoon virgin coconut oil
3 garlic cloves
1 can tomatoes
1 tablespoon mixed herbs
2 tablespoon chia seeds
1 tablespoon Barbecue Sauce (see
   Sauces)
1 tablespoon tomato paste
1 tablespoon Tomato Sauce
   (see Sauces)
salt and pepper
1 tablespoon virgin coconut oil

To make the pastry, process flour, salt, baking powder and butter together until a crumble is formed. Slowly add cold water until it forms a dough.

Roll in plastic wrap and refrigerate for 30 minutes.

Roll the pastry on a floured chopping board. Divide into four pieces and roll. Line pastry base in a four-hole pie tin (or use a 8-hole muffin tin for mini pies). Keep pastry aside for the tops of the pies. Lay a piece of baking paper over the top of the pastry and fill with rice or dried beans. Blind bake for 15 minutes in 160°C/325°F oven.

Cook lentils and quinoa according to packet directions and drain well. Fry and sauté onion in coconut oil until golden. Add garlic, tomatoes, mixed herbs, chia seeds, sauces and paste. Add the lentils and quinoa. Stir well, bring to the boil and simmer for 5 minutes.

Allow to cool. Add to processor to blend.

Remove the rice and beans from the pastry cases. Spoon the filling into the pastry cases and put the tops on carefully. Brush the pastry tops with oil and bake for a further 15–20 minutes, being careful not to burn.

Chia Meat Burgers

400g/14oz beef mince
1 onion, chopped
1 cup breadcrumbs
1 cup parsley leaves
1 cup mint leaves
½ cup grated carrot
2 tablespoon chia seeds and 1 cup water
1 tablespoon Barbecue Sauce (see
    Sauces) plus extra for serving
1 tablespoon Tomato Sauce
    (see Sauces) plus extra for serving
virgin coconut oil for frying

Blend meat, onion, fresh herbs, carrots and chia together. Add the sauces.

Form small patties with your hands, and fry in coconut oil for approximately 8 minutes on each side.

Serve with Barbecue or Tomato Sauce on the side.

Desserts

These desserts are based on agave syrup, dates, cacao, coconut oil, cashew nuts, vanilla bean and other nutritious ingredients. They keep in the refrigerator, freeze well and are easy to prepare well in advance.

Lucia Apple Crumble

3 apples, peeled and cored, cut into
quarters
½ cup pitted dates
1 teaspoon vanilla essence
1½ cup oat flour
1 teaspoon cinnamon
2 cups rolled oats
½ cup ground almonds
$\frac{1}{3}$ cup grapeseed or flaxseed oil
2 tablespoons chia seeds
sliced bananas, to serve

Blend apples with ¾ cup water in a food processor until it reaches a sauce-like consistency. Set aside.

Blend dates with 2 tablespoons of water and vanilla essence in the processor until it forms a paste. Sieve oat flour and cinnamon into a bowl, stir in oats, add the date paste and rub into oat mixture with your hands to form a crumble (it should be quite dry at this point). Stir in ground almonds and chia, add the grapeseed oil, and rub into the mixture. The crumble should be now moist; add more oil if required.

Press half the mixture into a small baking tin, press down evenly and top with apple sauce. Top with crumble and press down firmly. Set in the refrigerator for at least an hour. Cut into squares and enjoy cold or hot.

Top with sliced bananas and a drizzle of maple syrup.

Apple crumble is great as an after school snack or dessert.

Chia Apple Pudding with Macadamia Cream

Serves 2

3 apples, peeled, cored and quartered
1 teaspoon cinnamon
2 tablespoons chia seeds
1 cup water
strawberries, sliced, to garnish

MACADAMIA CREAM
½ cup macadamia nuts, soaked for
    1 hour and drained
½ cup fresh coconut or 1 tablespoon
    virgin coconut oil
1 vanilla bean or 1 teaspoon vanilla
    essence
juice of 1 lemon
1 tablespoon agave syrup

Place apples in a saucepan, cover with water and bring to the boil until they soften. Add cinnamon and cool.

Place chia seeds in a bowl and cover with one cup of water. Set aside until a gel-like consistency forms. Add chia to apples and stir well.

To make Macadamia Cream, place macadamia nuts, coconut or coconut oil, vanilla essence or vanilla bean, lemon juice and agave in a food processor and blend well until smooth and creamy

Serve apples with macadamia cream topped with fresh strawberries.

Mango & Coconut Tartlets

Makes: 8 small tartlets

1 cup cashew nuts, soaked for 1–2 hours
  and drained
1 tablespoon virgin coconut oil
½ cup fresh dates
1 tablespoon agave syrup
1 mango

Blend cashew nuts, coconut oil, dates and agave in a food processor until it comes together.

Press into the holes of a 8-hole patty tin, making sure to press mixture up the sides. Put in freezer to set.

Blend mango until smooth and fill the cashew tart cases.

Chocolate Mousse & Chia Seed Ice-cream

Serves 12

3 bananas, frozen
2 fresh dates
1 tablespoon agave syrup
1 tablespoon cacao powder
2 tablespoons chia seeds
raspberries, to serve

Allow banana to sit for 3 minutes on the bench.

Peel and slice banana and blend with dates, agave, cacoa and chia seeds.

Blend for 5 minutes or until smooth and creamy.

Serve in small ramekin dishes with raspberries, or on its own.

Frozen bananas are a better consistency for this dish. Raw, organic cacao powder is natural and unprocessed, and is rich in antioxidant flavanoids. It is derived from the mayhan tree in South America and comes as a cacao bean. I like to use the powder for most of the dessert recipes.

Chia Chocolates

Makes 12

2 tablespoons virgin coconut oil
2 tablespoons cacao powder
2 tablespoons chia seeds
2 tablespoons agave or honey
2 tablespoons mixed seeds
pinch salt

Melt the coconut oil in a saucepan. Pour into a bowl, add other ingredients and mix. Spoon into cupcake patties. Freeze overnight. Will keep for a week.

Vanilla Chia Chocolates

Makes 12

3 tablespoons virgin coconut oil
2 tablespoons cacao powder
2 tablespoons agave syrup or honey
1 teaspoon vanilla essence
2 tablespoons chia seeds

Melt the coconut in a saucepan, pour into a bowl, and add all other ingredients. Mix to combine, then spoon into cupcake patties. Freeze overnight.

Chia Chocolate Mousse

Serves 4

2 large avocados, pitted and cubed
¼ cup raw honey or agave syrup
3 tablespoons cacao powder
1 teaspoon vanilla extract
2 cups frozen mixed berries
2 tablespoons chia seeds
pinch of sea salt
mango, to serve

Blend avocado, honey, cacao and vanilla extract until smooth. Check flavour and add more agave or cacao if need be.

Allow berries to sit on a bench for 5 minutes. Blend berries and chia seeds together well and blend again into the cacao mixture. Serve in small ramekin dishes with slices of mango.

Flourless Chia Chocolate Cake

Serves 12

1 tablespoon chia seeds
½ cup hot water
½ cup cacao powder
2 tablespoons raw brown sugar
1 cup almond meal
3 eggs, separated
fresh berries, to serve
Macadamia Cream (see Sauces)

Preheat oven to 200°C/400°F. Add the chia seeds to the hot water and allow to sit for 3 minutes. In a large bowl, mix dry ingredients. Add chia mix and egg yolks, and mix well.

Whisk egg whites in a blender or beat until fluffy. Slowly fold egg whites into the mixture and pour into a small (10cm/6in) round cake tin.

Place tin in a baking pan filled with boiling water until it reaches up to 2/3 of the sides of the cake tin. Bake for approximately 30 minutes or until a skewer inserted into the middle of the cake comes out clean.

Cut into wedges and serve with fresh berries and Macadamia Cream.

Flourless chocolate cake is low in carbohydrates and gluten-free.

Strawberry Cakes

Makes 4

2 tablespoons chia seeds
2 tablespoons rice milk
1 red or pink lady apple
6 fresh dates
10 strawberries
1 tablespoon agave syrup

Mix the chia seeds and rice milk together and set aside until it forms a gel consistency.

Blend chia, apple and 5 dates in a food processor until tiny chunks form. Place apple mixture into 4 patty cases.

Blend 5 strawberries with 1 date and agave until smooth and creamy

Pour strawberry mixture into the patty cases. Freeze until solid. Slice remaining strawberries and place on top. You can also sprinkle a little almond meal and cacao over the top.

Chia Rice Bubble Cakes

Makes 12

3 tablespoons virgin coconut oil
1 cup puffed millet or puffed quinoa
1 tablespoon cacao powder
1 tablespoon agave syrup
1 tablespoon chia seeds

Melt coconut oil in a saucepan. Pour into a bowl and mix in remaining ingredients.

Spoon into patty cases and freeze.

I loved the rice bubble cakes my mother used to make, how they used to set and taste. Today I get much satisfaction in re-creating a healthier version of this recipe for my girls, filled with nutritional value.

Chia Strawberry Tart

Serves 8

CRUST

1 cup almonds, soaked for 1–2 hours
   and drained
2 tablespoons chia seeds
1 tablespoon maple syrup
1 tablespoon virgin coconut oil
1 fresh date, blended with 1 teaspoon
   agave syrup (or use date paste)
pinch salt

FILLING

1 cup raw cashews, soaked 1 hour and
   drained
juice of 1 lemon
¼ cup agave syrup
1 generous tablespoon virgin coconut oil
1 tablespoon chia seeds
¼ cup water
1 teaspoon vanilla essence
¼ teaspoon nutritional yeast

250 g fresh strawberries, thinly sliced,
   to garnish
1 tablespoon chia seeds, to serve
3 mint leaves, to garnish

Make the crust. Process the soaked almonds until small crumbs form. Place in a large bowl with remaining ingredients. Mix well with a spoon and press out with your hands into a 15cm/10in flan dish. Press well up the sides.

Blend all filling ingredients for 5 minutes until extra smooth and creamy. Pour mixture onto the crust and place in freezer for 30 minutes or until ready to serve.

Before serving, place the sliced strawberries around the top of the tart in whatever pattern you like. Sprinkle with extra chia seeds and add mint leaves for garnish.

Nutritional yeast is a deactivated yeast, sold in flakes or as powder. It's a Vitamin B boost you can add to soups and breads.

Citrus Chia Mini Cheesecakes

Makes 6

CRUST

1 cup shredded coconut

1 tablespoon chia seeds

½ cup flaxseed meal

½ cup quinoa flakes

pinch salt

1 tablespoon maple syrup

1 tablespoon virgin coconut oil

1 tablespoon agave syrup

1 tablespoon date paste (1 fresh date
   and 1 teaspoon agave syrup, blended)

FILLING

1 cup cashews, soaked 1 hour and
   drained

1 cup macadamia nuts, soaked 1 hour

1 cup lemon juice

3 tablespoons agave syrup

1 tablespoon maple syrup

1 dessertspoon vanilla essence

3 tablespoons virgin coconut oil, melted

½ large lemon, zested

1 tablespoon chia seeds

1 lemon, zested

¼ cup macadamias, roughly chopped

Make the crust by mixing all the ingredients together with a spoon and, using clean hands, pressing the mixture into cupcake patty tins. Press well up the sides. Place in freezer.

To make the filling, place all the filling ingredients in a food processor and blend until smooth.

Remove the tray from the freezer and pour in the filling.

Sprinkle the mini cheesecakes with lemon zest and chopped macadamias and serve immediately.

Chocolate Chia Tart

CRUST
3 tablespoons virgin coconut oil
1 cup cacao powder
½ cup oat flour
1 cup agave syrup
pinch sea salt
½ cup flax meal
2 tablespoons chia seeds

FILLING
½ cup cashew nuts, soaked and drained
½ cup water
3 tablespoon virgin coconut oil
½ cup cacao powder
¼ cup agave syrup
2 fresh dates
pinch of salt

raspberries or strawberries, to serve

Mix all the crust ingredients together. Press out onto baking paper in a round dish or non-stick tart pan and chill in freezer overnight.

Blend all filling ingredients in the processor until very smooth. Spoon into the crust and freeze overnight.

Serve sliced into squares on its own or with fresh raspberries or strawberries. Keeps well in the freezer in plastic wrap for a week.

Lemon & Chia Tartlets

Makes 12

CRUST

2 tablespoons virgin coconut oil

2 cups raw cashew nuts, soaked and
    drained

2 tablespoons agave syrup or honey

2 fresh dates

1 tablespoon chia seeds

pinch salt

FILLING

1 cup cashews, soaked for 1–2 hours
    and drained

1 cup macadamia nuts, soaked for 1–2
    hours and drained

1 cup lemon juice

3 tablespoons agave syrup

1 tablespoon maple syrup

1 dessertspoon vanilla essence

3 tablespoons virgin coconut oil

zest of ½ large lemon

1 tablespoon chia seeds

In a saucepan, melt coconut oil and pour into a food processor with other crust ingredients. Blend well, then press into a 12-hole cupcake tray, pressing evenly up the sides. Put the tray in the freezer overnight.

Place filling ingredients in a food processor and blend until smooth. Take tray out of freezer and pour in the filling. Place in the refrigerator for 1 hour before serving.

My favourite dessert when I was younger was lemon meringue pie and my girlfriend still likes to give this to me each year on my birthday. The problem is I don't know how to say no! So I created this healthy raw version that reminds me of lemon meringue... the tangy filling will leave you smiling.

Goji & Chia Soufflé

Serves 6

1 cup goji berries, soaked 15 minutes

1 cup cashew nuts, soaked for 1–2 hours and drained

½ cup agave syrup

1 cup water

1 tablespoon lemon juice

2 tablespoons raisins

1 teaspoon ginger powder

1 teaspoon lemon zest

1 tablespoon chopped orange

1 teaspoon vanilla essence

¼ cup virgin coconut oil

1 tablespoon chia seeds

1 tablespoon Macca powder

Raspberry Jam, to serve (see Breakfast)

Blend soaked goji berries first. Blend all remaining ingredients in food processor until really smooth.

Pour into soufflé dishes or a silicon tin and freeze.

Top with Raspberry Jam.

Lucia Choc-chia Brownie

Makes 12 squares

2 eggs
100g/3½oz butter, melted
½ cup cacao powder
½ cup raw brown sugar
1 tablespoon honey
2 tablespoons chia seeds
1 cup gluten-free plain/all purpose flour
¼ cup dark chocolate chips

Preheat oven to 160°C/320°F. Lightly beat eggs in a large bowl and mix in remaining ingredients, except chocolate chips, stirring well.

Pour out in a 15cm/10in shallow flan dish and sprinkle chocolate chips on top. Bake for 20–30 minutes or until cracks appear on the top, which indicates it is ready. Cool and cut into 12 squares.

A quick and easy recipe ideal for school lunches, a quick dessert or afternoon tea treat. Afternoon tea is often a big deal at our place, with the girls involved in creating a new recipe. Chia seeds add a nutritional element to a sweet treat.

Pecan & Chia Chocolate

Serves 4

1 cup pecan nuts
½ cup cacao powder
1 tablespoon maple syrup
2 tablespoons chia seeds
1 cup dark chocolate, melted
strawberries, to serve

Chop pecans in a food processor until small crumbs are formed, being careful not to overblend. Add to a large bowl.

Add cacao, maple syrup and chia seeds to melted chocolate and mix through. Pour melted chocolate mixture over the pecans and cool. Serve with sliced strawberries.

Chia Cookies

2 cups oat flour
1 cup cashew flour
¼ cup chia seeds
½ cup cacao powder
¼ cup water
½ cup agave
1 tablespoon vanillia
1 teaspoon sea salt
½ cup dark chocolate chips

Preheat oven to 160°C/320°F.

Mix all ingredients in a large bowl, stirring in the chocolate chips last.

Cover a baking tray with baking paper and drop teaspoonfuls of the mixture on to the tray.

Bake for 15–20 minutes and press choc chips on top.

You can also add dark chocolate chips on top for the kids.

Beetroot & Chocolate Chia Cake

1 egg
50g/1¾oz butter
¾ cup brown sugar
1 large raw beetroot, chopped
2 tablespoons cacao powder
1 cup almond meal
1 cup oat flour
1 cup quinoa flour or spelt flour
1 tablespoon chia seeds
juice of 1 orange

ICING
1 cup icing sugar
1 tablespoon cacao or cocoa powder
1 tablespoon butter
1 tablespoon hot water

Preheat oven to 140°C/280°F.

Lightly beat egg in a large bowl. Add butter, sugar and cream together well. In a food processor, blend raw beetroot and cacao together. Add to bowl with egg mixture, add almond meal, flours, chia seeds, and orange juice. Mix well into a cake batter, adding a little rice milk if the mixture is too dry. Pour into a shallow 15cm/10in flan dish and bake for 20–30 minutes until cooked. Cool on a tray.

To make the icing, mix all the ingredients in a bowl and spread onto the cake once cooled.

Cut cake into squares, like a fudge brownie.

When I was growing up, my Nana Barnes lived next door and she was a terrific baker. Every day there would be something new on her old coal range stove. Her cakes were always light and fluffy. This is a flat cake but a little icing on top and the taste of the beetroot and chocolate gives it a distinctive flavour.

Mixed Berry & Chia Chocolates

3 tablespoons virgin coconut oil
2 tablespoons cacao powder
2 tablespoons agave syrup
2 tablespoons chia seeds
pinch salt
½ cup blueberries, to serve
½ cup fresh strawberries, to serve

Melt coconut oil in a small saucepan, then add to a bowl with cacoa, agave, chia and salt. Stir well and pour small amounts into silicone cupcake patties.

Freeze until solid.

Serve with mixed berries.

It certainly is rewarding seeing my girls grow up in the greatest health and with an abundant supply of energy. The girls love how the seeds set at the bottom of the chocolates and are crunchy when they eat them.

Chia & Parsley Scones

Makes 6

1 egg, lightly beaten
½ cup grapeseed oil
1 cup rice milk
1 tablespoon maple syrup
1 cup tasty cheese
½ cup parsley
1 cup quinoa flour
1 cup self-raising/spelt flour
2 tablespoons chia seeds
1 teaspoon baking powder
Raspberry Jam, to serve (see Breakfast)

Preheat oven to 150°C/300°F. In a large bowl, combine beaten egg, grapeseed oil, rice milk, maple syrup, cheese and parsley.

Sift flours, chia seeds, and baking powder and add to the ingredients. Fold through and spoon out large amounts on baking paper on an oven tray. Bake until golden brown for approximately 15 minutes.

Top with Raspberry Jam.

Cheese eaten in moderation can have its benefits too. Full fat cheese is going to keep you full for longer and can be a great source of calcium.

Chia & Banana Cake

Serves 8

1 tablespoon butter

2 eggs, beaten

3 ripe bananas, mashed

3 tablespoons honey

1 teaspoon nutmeg

2 cups wholemeal flour

½ teaspoon baking powder

1 teaspoon cinnamon

2 tablespoons chia seeds

1 cup mixed seeds (sesame, pumpkin, sunflower)

½ cup raisins

¼ cup rice milk

juice of 1 orange

plain or Greek yoghurt, to serve

raspberries, fresh or frozen, to serve

Preheat oven to 180°C/360°F. Soften butter at room temperature, then combine with beaten eggs, mashed banana, honey and nutmeg,

Sift flour, baking powder, cinnamon, chia seeds and add to banana mixture. Add seeds, raisins, rice milk and orange juice and fold in gently until well mixed, adding more orange juice if required.

Pour batter into a lined loaf tin and bake for 20–25 minutes. Serve warm or cold, with yoghurt and raspberries.

Chocolate Truffles

Serves 12

1 cup almonds
2 tablespoons cacao powder
2 tablespoons agave syrup
3 fresh dates, or extra agave syrup
1 tablespoon water
1 tablespoon chia seeds

Blend all ingredients, except 1 tablespoon of cacao powder, in a food processor until well combined. Roll into little balls.

Place 1 tablespoon cacao in a bowl and roll balls in the cacao as a chocolate dusting.

Freeze until solid. Delicious served with fresh strawberries or on its own with a green tea.

Visit my home and you will always find a chocolate ball in the freezer. When I started my raw food journey I thought I was on to a winner when I drank my green smoothies and could enjoy a chocolate treat anytime. Fuelling the body with plenty of greens keeps the cravings away, but to know you can enjoy a little chocolate when you feel like it as a healthy snack for me is enjoying life and never feeling restricted or on a diet.

Vanilla-almond Chia Macarons

1 tablespoon chia seeds
1 cup almonds
½ cup oat flour
½ cup quinoa flakes
1 tablespoon vanilla essence
1 fresh date
¾ cup maple syrup
1 tablespoon virgin coconut oil
pinch sea salt
1 cup desiccated coconut

Mix all ingredients in a food processor until chunky, being careful not to overblend; the mixture should come together nicely without being too smooth.

Roll into medium balls, sprinkle coconut flakes on top and refridgerate until solid. Place in cupcake patties or on a plate. Can be frozen.

Chocolate Ginger Chia Macaroons

1 tablespoon chia seeds
1 cup macadamia nuts
¾ cup raw raw organic cacao powder
½ cup maple syrup
1 fresh date
1 tablespoon virgin coconut oil
1 tablespoon ginger ground
1 teaspoon vanilla essence
pinch salt
1 cup desiccated coconut

Mix all ingredients in a food processor until chunky, being careful not to overblend; the mixture should come together nicely without being too smooth.

Roll into medium balls, sprinkle coconut flakes on top and refrigerate until solid. Place in cupcake patties. Can be frozen.

Spreads, Sauces & Dressings

Spreads can be enjoyed with raw vegetables, crackers, on toast or bread. Many of these recipes are based around cashew nuts.

I'm often inspired to make my own sauces and display them in funky bottles.

Tomato Ginger Chia Sauce

Makes 1 cup

½ cup sundried tomatoes
1 tomato, diced
1 spring onion/scallion, chopped
juice of 1 lemon
¼ cup olive oil
1 teaspoon salt
1 tablespoon fresh ginger, soaked in
   ¼ cup hot water
pinch chili flakes
1 tablespoon chia seeds

Blend all ingredients until smooth.

Great with any salad and in pizza.

Almond Butter

Makes 1 cup

1 cup almonds, soaked for 1–2 hours
   and drained
2 tablespoons chia seeds
½ cup flaxseed oil
pinch of sea salt

Blend all ingredients until smooth.

Use as a spread or butter substitute.

Cashew Chia Butter

1 cup cashew nuts, soaked for 1–2 hours
   and drained
¼ cup chia seeds
1 teaspoon agave syrup
pinch salt

Blend in a food processor for 5 minutes, or until mixture forms a smooth nut butter.

A great spread for toast, sandwiches or pancakes.

Cashew Chia Cream

Makes 1 cup

1 cup raw cashew nuts, soaked for 1–2
   hours and drained
1 tablespoon chia seeds
juice of 1 lemon
pinch sea salt
1 teaspoon agave syrup
1 tablespoon olive oil
¼ cup water

Blend all ingredients for 5 minutes or until smooth and creamy.

Serve with raw vegetable batons, such as celery, carrot and capsicum, or use as a dip on crackers. If you like, add more water and use it as a dressing for salads.

Thai Chia Dressing

Makes 2 cups

½ cup chia seeds

½ cup sesame oil

½ cup soy sauce

½ cup olive oil

½ cup lime juice

1 tablespoon maple syrup

2 Thai chilies, deseeded and sliced or
   1½ teaspoon chili flakes

1 teaspoon sea salt

¼ cup cashew nuts, soaked for 1–2
   hours and drained

Blend all ingredients until smooth.

Great with salads, rice and as a seafood dipping sauce.

Macadamia Cream

Makes 1 cup

½ cup macadamia nuts soaked 1–2
    hours and drained
½ cup fresh coconut, or virgin
    coconut oil
1 teaspoon vanilla essence
juice of 1 lemon
1 tablespoon agave syrup.

Place all ingredients in a food processor and blend well until smooth and creamy.

Great with salads, dips and apple pie.

Chia Sour Cream

Makes 1 cup

½ cup raw cashews, soaked for 2 hours
    and drained
1 teaspoon apple cider vinegar
juice of ½ lemon
3–5 teaspoons water, depending on how
    thick you like your sour cream
pinch of salt
1 tablespoon chia seeds

Blend all ingredients except water. Slowly add water until it reaches your desired consistency.

Great with salads, dips and tacos.

Macadamia Ricotta

Makes 1 cup

1 cup macadamia nuts, soaked for 1–2
   hours and drained
juice of 1 lemon
2 tablespoons water
$^1/_3$ cup virgin coconut oil
¾ teaspoon salt
1 teaspoon nutritional yeast
1 tablespoon chia seeds

Place all ingredients in a food processor and blend until smooth.

Great with dips.

Macadamia Crumble

Makes 1 cup

½ cup macadamia nuts, soaked for 1–2
   hours and drained
1 tablespoon soy or almond milk
pinch of salt

Place all ingredients in a food processor and blend until large crumbs form.

Great with salads and macaroni cheese.

Lemon Mint Yoghurt

Makes 2 cups

1 cup cashew nuts, soaked for 1–2 hours
  and drained
¼ cup fresh coconut
⅓ cup water
juice of 2 lemons
zest of 1 lemon
½ cup fresh mint
1 tablespoon fresh mixed herbs
1 tablespoon chia seeds

Blend all ingredients in a food processor until smooth and creamy. Store in the refrigerator 3–4 days.

Serve with salad or crispbreads or use as a spread on chia crispbread.

Jay's Mayonnaise

Makes 2 cups

1 cup cashew nuts, soaked for 1–2 hours
  and drained
½ lemon
1 teaspoon apple cider vinegar
½ teaspoon sea salt
1 tcaspoon agave syrup
1 tablespoon chia seeds
1 teaspoon olive oil

Place all ingredients in a processor and blend until smooth and creamy.

Great with salads.

Basil Rocket Pesto

Makes 2 cups

1 cup fresh basil leaves
½ packed cup rocket/arugula leaves
½ cup raw pistachio nuts, shelled
1 tablespoon chia seeds
2 tablespoons olive oil
½ teaspoon sea salt
pinch cracked pepper

Place all ingredients in a food processor and blend until chunky.

Great with bruschetta, toast, crispbreads and raw vegetables.

Mint Basil Pesto

Makes 2 cups

½ cup packed basil
1 cup fresh mint
¼ cup pine nuts
2 tablespoons olive oil
1 tablespoon chia seeds
½ teaspoon sea salt
pinch black cracked pepper

Blend in a food processor well until smooth.

Great with bruschetta, toast, crispbreads and raw vegetables.

Avocado Chia Spread

1 avocado, pitted
1 green onion/salad onion, chopped
1 tablespoon white chia seeds
1 tablespoon olive oil
juice of 1 lemon
sea salt and pepper to taste

Place all ingredients in a food processor and blend until smooth.

A quick and easy snack or a spread. High in healthy fats and omega-3 and ever-so-tasty and satisfying.

Great with bruschetta, toast, crispbreads and raw vegetables.

Onion Chutney

1 tablespoon chia seeds
1 onion, chopped
1 chili, seeded and chopped
1 green capsicum/pepper chopped
1 lemon
2 tablespoons maple syrup

Blend ingredients in a food processor until chunky. Allow to sit for 2 days in a glass jar in the fridge before serving.

Great as a dip, with crispbreads and with vegetables.

Tomato Sauce (Ketchup)

Makes 1 bottle

2 tablespoons chia seeds
½ punnet cherry tomatoes, chopped
2 large tomatoes, chopped
½ red/Spanish onion chopped
¼ cup sundried tomatoes
2 fresh dates, stone removed
1 tablespoon balsamic dressing
1 teaspoon oregano

Blend ingredients in a food processor until smooth. Store in a glass jar. Will keep well for 3 days in the fridge.

Great with wedges, chips, pasta, as a pizza base and with meat dishes.

Barbecue Sauce 2

1 onion, chopped
1 tablespoon chia seeds
1 fresh date
½ cup sundried tomato
1 tomato
pinch salt

Blend ingredients in a food processor until smooth. Store in a glass jar. Will keep well for 3 days in the fridge.

Use this for pizza bases and meat dishes.

Raspberry Sauce

1 cup frozen raspberries
$1/3$ cup agave syrup
1 cup water
2 teaspoons chia seeds

Allow raspberries to thaw. Blend ingredients in a food processor until smooth. Store in a glass jar. Goes well with chocolate mousse (see recipe)

Great with ice cream.

Chocolate Chia Sauce

2 teaspoons chia seeds
2 tablespoons cacao
$1/4$ cup agave syrup
1 drop vanilla essence
$1/3$ teaspoon sea salt

Stir all ingredients well and store in a clean glass jar in the fridge.

Great with ice cream and frozen berries.

INDEX of RECIPES

Paperback edition published in 2013.

First published in 2013 by
New Holland Publishers Pty Ltd
London • Cape Town • Sydney • Auckland

The Chandlery Unit 114 50 Westminster Bridge Road London SE1 7QY
Wembley Square First Floor Solan Road Gardens Cape Town 8001 South Africa
1/66 Gibbes Street Chatswood NSW 2067 Australia
218 Lake Road Northcote Auckland New Zealand

www.newhollandpublishers.com

A record of this book is held at the British Library and the National Library of Australia

ISBN 9781742574769

Publisher: Linda Williams
Editor: Lliane Clarke
Designer: Tracy Loughlin
Photographs: Graeme Gillies
Food stylist: Nicky Arthur and Audrey Lewis
Proofreader: Vicky Fisher
Production director: Olga Dementiev
Printer: Toppan Leefung Printing Ltd (China)

10 9 8 7 6 5 4 3 2 1

Keep up with New Holland Publishers on Facebook
www.facebook.com/NewHollandPublishers

Keep up with Nicky Arthur at nickyarthur.com

UK £12.99
US $19.99